Wa   I0019454

Privacy and Practicality of Identity Management Systems

Waleed Alrodhan

Privacy and Practicality of Identity Management Systems

Academic Overview

VDM Verlag Dr. Müller

Impressum/Imprint (nur für Deutschland/ only for Germany)

Bibliografische Information der Deutschen Nationalbibliothek: Die Deutsche Nationalbibliothek verzeichnet diese Publikation in der Deutschen Nationalbibliografie; detaillierte bibliografische Daten sind im Internet über http://dnb.d-nb.de abrufbar.

Alle in diesem Buch genannten Marken und Produktnamen unterliegen warenzeichen-, marken- oder patentrechtlichem Schutz bzw. sind Warenzeichen oder eingetragene Warenzeichen der jeweiligen Inhaber. Die Wiedergabe von Marken, Produktnamen, Gebrauchsnamen, Handelsnamen, Warenbezeichnungen u.s.w. in diesem Werk berechtigt auch ohne besondere Kennzeichnung nicht zu der Annahme, dass solche Namen im Sinne der Warenzeichen- und Markenschutzgesetzgebung als frei zu betrachten wären und daher von jedermann benutzt werden dürften.

Coverbild: www.ingimage.com

Verlag: VDM Verlag Dr. Müller GmbH & Co. KG
Dudweiler Landstr. 99, 66123 Saarbrücken, Deutschland
Telefon +49 681 9100-698, Telefax +49 681 9100-988
Email: info@vdm-verlag.de
Zugl.: London, Royal Holloway, University of London, 2010

Herstellung in Deutschland:
Schaltungsdienst Lange o.H.G., Berlin
Books on Demand GmbH, Norderstedt
Reha GmbH, Saarbrücken
Amazon Distribution GmbH, Leipzig
ISBN: 978-3-639-38025-5

Imprint (only for USA, GB)

Bibliographic information published by the Deutsche Nationalbibliothek: The Deutsche Nationalbibliothek lists this publication in the Deutsche Nationalbibliografie; detailed bibliographic data are available in the Internet at http://dnb.d-nb.de.

Any brand names and product names mentioned in this book are subject to trademark, brand or patent protection and are trademarks or registered trademarks of their respective holders. The use of brand names, product names, common names, trade names, product descriptions etc. even without a particular marking in this works is in no way to be construed to mean that such names may be regarded as unrestricted in respect of trademark and brand protection legislation and could thus be used by anyone.

Cover image: www.ingimage.com

Publisher: VDM Verlag Dr. Müller GmbH & Co. KG
Dudweiler Landstr. 99, 66123 Saarbrücken, Germany
Phone +49 681 9100-698, Fax +49 681 9100-988
Email: info@vdm-publishing.com

Printed in the U.S.A.
Printed in the U.K. by (see last page)
ISBN: 978-3-639-38025-5

This page has been intentionally left blank.

This page has been intentionally left blank.

Contents

11

CONTENTS

List of Figures

List of Tables

Abbreviations

AAPML:	Attribute Authority Policy Markup Language
AAS:	Attribute Authority Service
AES:	Advanced Encryption Standard
API:	Application Programming Interface
ARP:	Attribute Release Policy
AS:	Authentication Service
ASN.1:	Abstract Syntax Notation One
CA:	Certification Authority
CARML:	Client Attribute Requirements Markup Language
CDC:	Common Domain Cookie
CDM:	Context Data Model
CEUA:	CardSpace-Enabled User Agent
CoT:	Circle of Trust
CS-E:	CardSpace-Enabled
CSP:	Credentials Service Provider
DHKE:	Diffie-Hellman Key Exchange
DNS:	Domain Name System
DNSSec:	Domain Name System Security Extensions
DOM:	Document Object Model
DRM:	Digital Rights Management
DTD:	Document Type Definition
DS:	Discovery Service

DSA: Digital Signature Algorithm

DSS: Digital Signature Standard

EPR: Endpoint Reference

GUI: Graphical User Interface

HoK: Holder-of-Key

HTML: Hypertext Mark-up Language

HTTP: Hypertext Transfer Protocol

HTTPS: Hypertext Transfer Protocol Secure

ICIM: Information Card-based Identity Management

ID: Identity

IdAS: Identity Attribute Service

ID-FF: Identity Federation Framework

IdP: Identity Provider

ID-SIS: Identity Service Interface Specification

ID-WSF: Identity Web Services Framework

IETF: Internet Engineering Task Force

IP: Internet Protocol

IPsec: Internet Protocol Security

IRI: Internationalized Resource Identifier

JISC: Joint Information Systems Committee

L-E: Liberty-Enabled

LEC: Liberty-Enabled Client

LEUA: Liberty-Enabled User Agent

LoA: Level of Assurance

MAC: Message Authentication Code

NIST: Institute of Standards and Technology

OECD: Organisation for Economic Co-operation and Development

OMB: Office of Management and Budget

P3P:	Platform for Privacy Preferences Project
PC:	Personal Computer
PGP:	Pretty Good Privacy
PHP:	PHP: Hypertext Preprocessor
PII:	Personally Identifiable Information
PIV:	Personal Identity Verification
PID:	Persistent Identifier
PPID:	Private Personal Identifier
RIPEMD:	RACE Integrity Primitives Evaluation Message Digest
PKI:	Public Key Infrastructure
PoA:	Proof of Authenticity
RP:	Relying Party
RSA:	Rivest-Shamir-Adleman
RST:	Request Security Token
RSTR:	Request Security Token Response
SAML:	Security Assertion Markup Language
SHA:	Secure Hash Algorithm
ShARPE:	Shibboleth Attribute Release Policy Editor
SIP:	Self-issued Identity Provider
SIT:	Secured from Identity Theft
SMS:	Short Message Service
SP:	Service Provider
SSH:	Secure Shell
SSL:	Secure Sockets Layer
SSO:	Single Sign-On
STS:	Security Token Service
TLS:	Transport Layer Security
TTP:	Trusted Third Party

UDI:	Universal Data Identifier
UDR:	Uniform Data Reference
URI:	Uniform Resource Identifier
URL:	Uniform Resource Locator
USB:	Universal Serial Bus
W3C:	World-Wide Web Consortium
WAYF:	Where Are You From
WinFX:	Windows .NET Framework Extension
WS:	Web Services
WSDL:	Web Services Description Language
XACML:	eXtensible Access Control Markup Language
XHTML:	eXtensible Hypertext Markup Language
XML:	eXtensible Markup Language
XRDS:	eXtensible Resource Descriptor Sequence
XRI:	eXtensible Resource Identifier

Introduction

Contents

In Section 1.1 of this introductory chapter we outline the research motivation of this thesis. We describe the main contributions of the thesis in Section 1.2, and its structure in Section 1.3. Finally, a list of publications is provided in Section 1.4.

1.1 Motivation

The growing reliance on Internet applications and services has made it common, or even necessary, for Internet users to possess multiple digital identities. The task of managing these identities is a challenging problem for both users and service providers. Moreover, protecting users' privacy and their identifying information has become a very serious concern because of the rapid growth in identity theft and other criminal attacks in the last few years. According to an Identity Theft Resource Center (ITRC)[1] report, the number of identity information theft incidents reported to the center in the first half of 2008 was 69% greater than the number of reported incidents during the same period in 2007.

---

[1] http://www.idtheftcenter.org

Identity management systems aim to facilitate the task of identity management and to ease the control of identity information for authorised entities, as well as helping to preserve user privacy. The last few years have witnessed a significant growth in the number of identity management systems, and this number is expected to grow further in the next few years. An RNCOS[2] report [156] predicts that the identity management market will grow at a compound annual growth rate of nearly 23% between 2009 and 2012. The vast majority of these identity management systems are not interoperable, and implementation and privacy issues remain. This thesis aims to enhance the privacy and practicality of identity management systems.

The lack of interoperability between identity management systems is likely to be a serious obstacle to their practical use. One reason for this is that most recently proposed identity management solutions (including Federated identity and Information Card-based schemes) require several independent entities to participate in the identification and/or authentication process. Moreover, the practicality of identity management systems can be enhanced by improving their flexibility, and enabling the development of identity-based services. Identity-based services are services that can be used to retrieve information about an identity, update information about an identity, or perform an action for the benefit of the owner of an identity [64]. In this thesis we propose a novel scheme enabling the integration of two of the most widely discussed identity management systems, namely Microsoft CardSpace (an Information Card-based identity management system) and the Liberty Alliance Project (a Federated identity management scheme). We also propose a delegation service framework for the Liberty Alliance project. This framework takes advantage of the trust relationships that exist by definition within the Liberty Alliance circles of trust, and involves the use of delegation assertions that can be built using the Security Assertion Mark-up Language (SAML) version 2 standard.

---

[2]http://www.rncos.com

With regard to privacy, we outline a number of security vulnerabilities in Information Card-based identity management systems. We then propose solutions to these vulnerabilities, which mitigate the risk of privacy violation. We also propose novel methods to enhance user authentication in Information Card-based identity management systems.

1.2 Summary of Contributions

This thesis proposes a number of novel schemes to enhance the privacy and practicality of identity management systems. The main contributions of this thesis are as follows.

- A scheme is proposed which enhances the privacy of Information Card-based identity management systems by mitigating the risk of users being deceived by fake service providers (e.g. as might arise through phishing). The scheme also reduces the risk of an attacker impersonating a legitimate user to access services offered by one or more service providers, after having broken the only means employed to authenticate the user to identity provider. This can be achieved by addressing two security vulnerabilities of such systems, namely their reliance on user judgements of the honesty of service providers, and their reliance on a single layer of authentication. This scheme is based on the concept of SIT attributes. A number of other possible approaches to addressing the outlined security vulnerabilities are also described.

- Two methods are described which enhance user authentication in Information Card-based identity management systems. These methods mitigate the risk of service providers being deceived by untrustworthy identity providers, by imposing an additional and transparent authentication layer between the user and the service provider.

- An integration scheme enabling interoperation between the Liberty Alliance Project ID-WSF LEC SSO profile framework (a Federated identity management scheme) and the Microsoft CardSpace framework (an Information Card-based identity management system) is given.

- A delegation framework for Federated identity management systems is proposed. This framework is built on SAML 2.0 and Liberty ID-FF 1.2 single sign-on profiles, and supports both direct and indirect delegation.

1.3   Structure of Thesis

This thesis is divided into three parts, and is organised as follows.

Part I: provides an introduction to the security services and mechanisms used throughout the thesis. It also provides an overview of identity management and identity management systems. It contains three chapters, as follows.

- **Chapter 2:** This is a preliminary chapter, in which we provide definitions of the security services and mechanisms used throughout the thesis.

- **Chapter 3:** In this chapter we provide an overview of the concept of identity, and a number of related topics such as Levels of Assurance and Single Sign-On. We also describe in detail three of the most widely discussed identity management models, namely isolated, Information Card-based, and Federated identity management.

- **Chapter 4:** In this chapter we provide a detailed description of five web-based identity management systems, namely Microsoft CardSpace, Higgins, Liberty Alliance, Shibboleth, and OpenID. Additionally, we investigate the security problems arising in these systems. We then discuss the practicality of identity management systems, and how practicality can be enhanced by developing reliable integration and delegation schemes. This is followed by detailed reviews of the Project Concordia integration framework, the draft Shibboleth delegation framework, and the OAuth delegation framework; in addition we give a review of related literature.

Part II: proposes a number of novel approaches designed to enhance the privacy and practicality of identity management systems. It contains the following four chapters.

- **Chapter 5:** In this chapter we propose a scheme to address two security shortcomings in Information Card-based identity management systems, both of which could lead to a serious privacy violation. The proposed scheme is based on the concept of SIT attributes.

- **Chapter 6:** The growing number of identity theft techniques raises the risk of service providers being deceived by fake identity providers in an Information Card-based identity management framework. In this chapter we show how this risk can be mitigated by enhancing user authentication within Information Card-based identity management systems. Two independent methods that can be used to enhance user authentication are described.

- **Chapter 7:** In this chapter we propose an approach to enable interoperation between the Liberty Alliance Project ID-WSF LEC SSO profile (a Federated identity management scheme) and the Microsoft CardSpace framework (an Information Card-based identity management scheme). This integration scheme enhances the practicality of both schemes.

- **Chapter 8:** Building support for delegation services into a Federated identity management system enhances its flexibility and scalability. In this chapter we propose a delegation framework for such a system. The framework is built on the ID-WSF SAML 2.0 Single Sign On profiles, and supports both direct and indirect delegation.

Part III: concludes the thesis by summarising the main contributions and discussing possible future work. This part of the thesis consists of a single chapter, as follows.

- **Chapter 9:** This chapter summarises the thesis and gives some concluding remarks. It also discusses possible future research with the goal of enhancing identity management systems.

1.4 Publications

A list of publications describing some of the research outcomes contained in this thesis is provided below.

- W. A. Alrodhan and C. J. Mitchell. Addressing privacy issues in CardSpace. In *Proceedings of the Third International Symposium on Information Assurance and Security, IAS 2007, Manchester, UK*, pages 285-291. IEEE Computer Society, 2007.

- W. A. Alrodhan and C. J. Mitchell. A client-side CardSpace-Liberty integration architecture. In *Proceedings of the Seventh symposium on Identity and Trust on the Internet , IDTrust 2008, NIST, Gaithersburg, USA*, volume 283, pages 1-7. ACM International Conference Proceeding Series, 2008.

- W. A. Alrodhan and C. J. Mitchell. A delegation framework for Liberty. In *Proceedings of the Third Conference on Advances in Computer Security and*

Forensics, ACSF 2008, Liverpool, UK, pages 67-73. Liverpool John Moores University, 2008.

- W. A. Alrodhan and C. J. Mitchell. Improving the security of CardSpace. *EURASIP Journal on Information Security*, 9, 2009. Article ID 167216.

- W. A. Alrodhan and C. J. Mitchell. Enhancing user authentication in claim-based identity management. In *Proceedings of the 2010 International Symposium on Collaborative Technologies and Systems, CTS 2010, Chicago, Illinois, USA*, pages 75-83. IEEE, 2010.

- H. Al-Sinani, W. A. Alrodhan, and C. J. Mitchell. Liberty-CardSpace integration for CardSpace users. In *Proceedings of the ninth symposium on Identity and Trust on the Internet , IDTrust 2010, NIST, Gaithersburg, USA*, pages 12-25. ACM, 2010.

Part I

Background

Security Services and Mechanisms

Contents

In Sections 2.2 and 2.3 of this preliminary chapter we provide definitions of relevant security services and mechanisms. We also provide brief introductions to the security protocols used in this thesis in Section 2.4. These protocols include the Secure Sockets Layer (and Transport Layer Security), the Security Assertion Markup Language, the Web Services protocols, and the Diffie-Hellman Key Exchange protocol. Finally, an overview of Public Key Infrastructures is provided in Section 2.5.

2.1   Introduction

In order to understand the security techniques used in this thesis, definitions of fundamental security services and mechanisms must first be provided. In this chapter we provide brief definitions of these services and mechanisms. Many of the definitions have been derived from [56, 66, 84, 122, 160, 164]. We also provide brief introductions to the Secure Sockets Layer and Transport Layer Security (SSL/TLS), the Security Assertion Markup Language (SAML), Web Services protocols (WS-*), and Public Key Infrastructures (PKIs).

2.2   Security Services

In the context of the communication of electronic data, *security services* are the measures, or types of protection, needed to address identified threats to a system's security. Below we define the security services that are relevant to this thesis.

2.2.1 Data Confidentiality

This service provides protection of data against unauthorised disclosure by ensuring that it is accessible only to authorised individuals, entities or processes.

2.2.2 Data Integrity

This service counters active threats to the validity of transferred data. It provides protection against unauthorised alteration or destruction of data.

2.2.3 Access Control

This service provides protection of system resources against unauthorised use. This includes the use of a communications resource, and execution of a processing resource. It also includes reading, writing or deletion of an information resource.

Delegation

Delegation of access rights and/or privileges within a given system can be a necessary part of an access control system [71, 172]. Delegation enables an entity to delegate some or all of its rights to other entities in a specific domain [18]. For example, many Digital Rights Management (DRM) systems offer delegation services to consumers so that they can delegate their access rights to a protected piece of media to a number of devices [15, 143, 167]. Many Grid systems also incorporate delegation frameworks to enhance efficiency and scalability [7].

A wide variety of delegation models have been introduced in the literature (e.g.

[53, 178, 184]). There is no single agreed model, but there are many similarities between what we propose and those in the literature; we have tried to devise a general model which can be made consistent with the various existing schemes by, where necessary, combining roles. Perhaps the most similar models to that introduced here are those given in [5, 132, 148], although the precise terminology differs.

The following definitions for delegation-related terminology are used in this thesis:

- **Privilege:** A right to access specific resources or to perform certain tasks. A user may have a number of such privileges.

- **Delegation:** The act of (temporarily or permanently) transferring privileges from one entity to another.

- **Delegator:** An entity that transfers (delegates) all or a subset of its privileges to a Delegatee.

- **Delegatee:** An entity that receives all or a subset of the Delegator's privileges in order to use them on the Delegator's behalf.

- **Delegation Assertion:** An assertion of the correctness of, and authority for, a delegation, issued by a Delegation Authority to a Delegatee.

- **Delegation Authority:** An entity that controls delegation and issues delegation assertions.

- **Delegation Assertion Target (or Service Provider):** An entity that holds the resource to which access is to be delegated.

The *delegation authority* is the entity responsible for managing and issuing delegation assertions. In the delegation scheme described in Chapter 8, this role is played by an independent trusted party (e.g. an identity provider in an identity management system). However, in general, this role could be combined with that of the delegator itself.

In the delegation scheme described in Chapter 8, the delegation authority must get the explicit consent of the delegator to the delegation (either online or offline) before the requested *delegation assertion* is issued. The *delegator* may also want to impose certain conditions on the delegation (e.g. the delegation validity period, whether or not the delegation assertion is re-delegatable to another entity, the type of information that can be retrieved, etc.); these conditions must be stated in the delegation assertion. The *delegatee* must present the delegation assertion to the service provider in order to be granted the delegated *privileges*. Indeed, the service provider must trust the delegation assertion issuer (i.e. the delegation authority); otherwise it will reject the delegation assertion. Note that in the delegation scheme described in Chapter 8, the delegator does not delegate its privilege(s) to the delegation authority, nor does it forward a delegation assertion to the delegatee through the delegation authority. Instead, the delegator asks the delegation authority to generate a delegation assertion and send it to the delegatee, which can subsequently be used to access a protected resource at the service provider. Figure 2.1 shows the relationships between the roles in the delegation model.

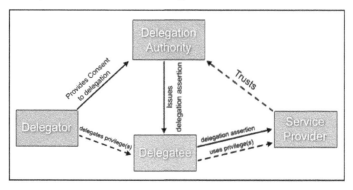

Figure 2.1: A conceptual delegation model

We also distinguish between two types of delegation, which we refer to as direct and indirect delegation (see for example [148, 176]). An instance of delegation is said to be *direct* if the delegatee specified by the delegator uses delegated privileges directly to achieve a task (e.g. obtaining specific data from an SP). However, if it turns out that the delegation assertion target (i.e. the SP) cannot deliver the requested service (or data) without first obtaining certain user-related data from another SP, then the delegation assertion target can play the role of a new delegatee and request a new (or revised) delegation assertion to be forwarded to a new SP. We refer to such a case as *indirect* delegation. Note that in this latter case, the delegation authority may be required to generate more than one set of delegation assertions, and that the SP in the previous delegation step will become a delegatee. Figure 2.2 shows the information flows for the two types of delegation.

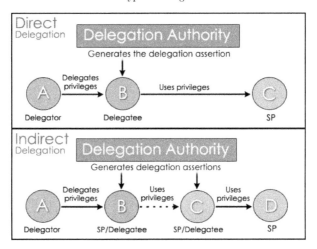

Figure 2.2: Direct and indirect delegation

2.2.4 Authentication

This service can be subdivided into two main types, namely entity authentication and data origin authentication.

An entity authentication service provides assurance to one entity that another entity is as claimed, and that it is not attempting to impersonate another entity. It also provides assurance that the current communications session is not an unauthorised replay of a previous connection. Although it is typically used at start of a connection, this service may also be used during a connection.

The data origin authentication service provides assurance to an entity that the source of received data is as claimed.

2.2.5 Non-Repudiation

This service provides an evidence concerning a claimed event or action in order to resolve disputes about the occurrence or non occurrence of the event or action [100]. Delivering such a service to an entity involves providing evidence to that entity regarding the action concerned, where this evidence must be of potential value to a third party.

This service has two cases of particular importance. The first is non-repudiation of origin, in which the recipient of data is provided with evidence of its origin. The second is non-repudiation of delivery, in which the sender of data is provided with evidence of its delivery.

2.2.6 Anonymity

This service provides assurance to a subject causing an action, that it is not identifiable within a set of subjects, called the anonymity set. The anonymity set is the set of all possible subjects which might have caused such an action [147].

Pseudonymity can be used to help provide an anonymity service. It involves the use of pseudonyms as identifiers for a subject, instead of the subject's actual identifier (e.g. the subject's name). One feature of pseudonymity is that it enables entities to collect additional data relating to a subject without having to know its identity [101]. Pseudonyms can be either temporary or permanent within a given system. A subject that is identified by a pseudonym is called the *holder* of that pseudonym [147].

2.2.7 Privacy

This service provides protection of the attributes, preferences, and traits associated with an individual's identities against unauthorised distribution or use [181].

2.2.7.1 The W3C Platform for Privacy Preferences Project

The World-Wide Web Consortium (W3C) Platform for Privacy Preferences Project (P3P)[1] enables web sites on the Internet to express their privacy practices in a standard format, the P3P Preference Exchange Language (APPEL) [117], so they can be retrieved and interpreted by user agents (i.e. P3P-enabled web browsers). APPEL is an XML-based language that can be used by a user to express her privacy preferences in the form of a set of preference-rules (called a ruleset). This ruleset

---

[1]http://www.w3.org/P3P

is then passed to the user agent which will automatically (or semi-automatically) inform users of the privacy practices of visited web sites (in both machine- and human-readable formats), and advise them accordingly.

A web site can use an XML-based *P3P policy* to represent its privacy-related practices, enumerate the types of data or data elements collected, and explain how the data will be used [179]. Each P3P policy is applied to specific web resources (e.g. web pages, images, cookies, etc.) listed in a policy reference file. P3P policies can also contain information about data recipients, dispute resolution, and the address of a web site's human-readable privacy policy. P3P user agents may be developed to test whether a web site's practices are compliant with a specific privacy law or code. Although P3P provides a technical mechanism for ensuring that users can be informed about the visited web sites privacy policies before they release personal information, it does not provide a technical mechanism for ensuring that web sites are acting according to their policies.

The P3P specifications define 16 categories of personal data that should be protected while visiting web sites over the Internet [179]. These categories are as follows.

- **Physical Contact Information**. Information that allows an individual to be contacted or located in the physical world, such as a telephone number or street address.

- **Online Contact Information**. Information that allows an individual to be contacted or located on the Internet, such as an email address. Often, this information is independent of the specific computer used to access the network.

- **Unique Identifiers**. Non-financial identifiers, excluding government-issued identifiers, issued for the purpose of consistently identifying or recognising an individual. These include identifiers issued by a web site or service.

- **Purchase Information**. Information actively generated by the purchase of a product or service, including information about the method of payment.

- **Financial Information.** Information about an individual's finances including account status and activity information such as account balance, payment or overdraft history, and information about an individual's purchases or use of financial instruments including credit or debit card information. Information which is just derived from a discrete purchase by an individual, as described in "Purchase Information", does not come under the definition of "Financial Information".

- **Computer Information.** Information about the computer system that the individual is using to access the network, such as the IP address, domain name, browser type or operating system.

- **Navigation and Click-stream Data.** Data passively generated by browsing a web site, such as which pages are visited, and how long a user stays on each page.

- **Interactive Data.** Data actively generated from, or reflecting explicit interactions with, a service provider through its site — such as queries to a search engine, or logs of account activity.

- **Demographic and Socioeconomic Data.** Data about an individual's characteristics, such as gender, age, and income.

- **Content.** The words and expressions contained in the body of a communication, such as the text of an email, bulletin board posting, or chat room communication.

- **State Management Mechanisms.** Mechanisms for maintaining a stateful session with a user, or automatically recognising users who have visited a particular site or accessed particular content previously, such as HTTP cookies.

- **Political Information.** Membership of, or affiliation with, groups such as religious organisations, trade unions, professional associations, political parties, etc.

- **Health Information**. Information about an individual's physical or mental health, sexual orientation, use of or inquiry into health care services or products, and purchase of health care services or products.

- **Preference Data**. Data about an individual's likes and dislikes, such as favourite colour or musical tastes.

- **Location Data**. Information that can be used to identify an individual's current physical location and track them as their location changes, such as GPS position data.

- **Government-issued Identifiers**. Identifiers issued by a government for the purpose of consistently identifying an individual.

- **Other**. Other types of (personal) data not captured by the above definitions.

2.2.7.2 OECD privacy guidelines

In 1980, the council of the Organisation for Economic Co-operation and Development (OECD) published guidelines on the protection of privacy and transborder flows of personal data [1]. These guidelines aim to *"harmonise national privacy legislation and, while upholding such human rights, would at the same time prevent interruptions in international flows of data"* [1]. Many of the user privacy laws now in place in a wide range of countries that govern the use of information systems are derived from the OECD privacy guidelines. These guidelines contain eight basic principles for personal data protection. They are as follows.

1. **Collection Limitation Principle**. There should be limits on the collection of personal data, and any such data should be obtained by lawful and fair means and, where appropriate, with the knowledge or consent of the data

subject.

2. **Data Quality Principle**. Personal data should be relevant to the purposes for which they are to be used, and, to the extent necessary for those purposes, should be accurate, complete and kept up-to-date.

3. **Purpose Specification Principle**. The purposes for which personal data are collected should be specified not later than at the time of data collection, and the subsequent use limited to the fulfilment of those purposes or such others as are not incompatible with those purposes and as are specified on each occasion of a change of purpose.

4. **Use Limitation Principle**. Personal data should not be disclosed, made available or otherwise used for purposes other than those specified at the time of collection except with the consent of the data subject or by the authority of law.

5. **Security Safeguards Principle**. Personal data should be protected by reasonable security safeguards against such risks as loss or unauthorised access, destruction, use, modification or disclosure of data.

6. **Openness Principle**. There should be a general policy of openness about developments, practices and policies with respect to personal data. Means should be readily available of establishing the existence and nature of personal data, and the main purposes of their use, as well as the identity and usual residence of the data controller.

7. **Individual Participation Principle**. An individual should have the right:
   a) to obtain from a data controller, confirmation of whether or not the data controller has data relating to him;
   b) to have communicated to him, data relating to him within a reasonable time, at a charge that is not excessive, in a reasonable manner, and in a form that is readily intelligible to him;
   c) to be given reasons if a request made under subparagraphs (a) and (b) is

denied, and to be able to challenge such denial; and

d) to challenge data relating to him and, if the challenge is successful, to have the data erased, rectified, completed or amended.

8. **Accountability Principle**. A data controller should be accountable for complying with measures which give effect to the principles stated above.

In this thesis, we use the above principles when evaluating the privacy properties of information systems. A system that fails to fairly satisfy the requirements of any of the OECD personal data protection principles is deemed vulnerable to privacy violation.

2.3 Security Mechanisms

In the context of the communication of electronic data, *security mechanisms* are the methods by which security services are provided [56, 84]. Below we describe the security mechanisms that are relevant to this thesis.

2.3.1 Symmetric Cryptography

Symmetric (or secret key) cryptography covers a range of types of mechanisms that can be used to provide security services. When using symmetric cryptography, the sender and receiver of a message must share a secret key. Establishing this secret key in a secure manner is one of the major issues in the use of symmetric cryptography.

Two of the most commonly used classes of symmetric cryptographic mechanisms are symmetric encryption schemes and message authentication code algorithms.

2.3.1.1 Symmetric Encryption

A symmetric encryption mechanism can be used to provide the data confidentiality service. In symmetric encryption, a message, m, is encrypted to produce a ciphertext, c. This process is reversible, so that this ciphertext, c, can be decrypted to produce the original message, m. The same secret key, k, is used for both encryption and decryption. There are two widely used types of symmetric encryption algorithms, namely block ciphers and stream ciphers. A block cipher algorithm operates on blocks of bits (typically of 64 or 128 bits in length), and such an algorithm can be used in a variety of ways (called modes of operation) to encrypt messages of arbitrary length. A stream cipher operates rather differently, and involves the use of a keystream generator to produce a pseudorandom sequence of bits, which is used to encrypt a message one bit at a time.

Examples of block ciphers include AES [139] and RC6 [153]. Symmetric encryption algorithms are standardised in ISO/IEC 18033-3 [93] and ISO/IEC 18033-4 [94].

2.3.1.2 Message Authentication Codes

A Message Authentication Code (MAC) algorithm is a symmetric cryptographic mechanism that can be used to provide both data origin authentication and data integrity services. A MAC is a cryptographic checksum of a message, m, and is computed using a secret key, k. The same secret key is used for both computing and verifying the MAC. For the purposes of this thesis, $MAC_k(m)$ denotes a MAC computed on a message m using a secret key k.

Examples of MAC functions include the CBC-MAC schemes [86] and HMAC [90, 141].

2.3.2 Asymmetric Cryptography

Unlike symmetric cryptographic mechanisms, asymmetric cryptographic techniques do not involve the use of a shared secret key. Instead, each participating entity must possess a matching pair of keys, one to be kept secret called the *private key*, and the other to be made available to other communicating parties called the *public key*. It must be computationally hard to deduce the private key from the public key. The roles of the keys depend on the type of asymmetric technique in use.

One major issue in the practical use of asymmetric cryptography is the distribution of the public key in a reliable manner. For this to be achieved, the authenticity and the integrity of the public key must be preserved. Many schemes have been designed to address this issue, including public key infrastructures (discussed in section 2.5), and webs of trust, as used by Pretty Good Privacy (PGP) [70].

2.3.2.1 Asymmetric Encryption

Asymmetric encryption mechanisms can be used to provide the data confidentiality service. In asymmetric encryption, a message, m, is encrypted using a public key, k_p, to produce a ciphertext, c. This process is reversible, so that this ciphertext, c, can be decrypted using a private key, k_s, that matches the public key to produce the original message m.

Examples of asymmetric encryption algorithms include Rivest-Shamir-Adleman (RSA) [154, 155], and ElGamal [69]. Asymmetric encryption algorithms are standardised in ISO/IEC 18033-2 [96].

2.3.2.2 Digital Signatures

Digital signatures can be used to provide data origin authentication, data integrity, and non-repudiation services. In order to use a digital signature scheme, an entity must possess a key pair. The private key (the *signing key*) is used for generating signatures, and the public key (the *verification key*) is used for verifying signatures. An entity, A, signs a message, m, using its signing key to generate a digital signature. This signature can then be verified by other entities using A's verification key.

Examples of digital signature algorithms include the RSA signature scheme [155], and the ElGamal signature scheme [69]. Digital signature techniques are standardised in ISO/IEC 9796 [89, 97], and ISO/IEC 14888 [95, 98, 99].

2.3.3 Cryptographic Hash Functions

A cryptographic hash function is a function, h, that maps a message, m, of any length to a fixed length output. This output is called a hash code or message digest. A cryptographic hash function should be easy to calculate.

A cryptographic hash function must satisfy the following three properties.

1. *First preimage resistance*: Given a hash code, d, it must be computationally infeasible to find a message, m, such that $h(m) = d$.

2. *Second preimage resistance*: Given a message, m, it must be computationally infeasible to find a second message, $m' \neq m$, such that $h(m) = h(m')$.

3. *Collision resistance*: It must be computationally infeasible to find any two distinct messages, m and m', such that $h(m) = h(m')$.

Cryptographic hash functions are an essential part of the computation of most practical digital signature schemes; a hash function can also be used to construct a MAC function, as in the HMAC scheme [90, 141]. Examples of cryptographic hash functions include SHA-1 [61, 91, 142], RIPEMD-160 [91] and Whirlpool [91]. Cryptographic hash functions are standardised in ISO/IEC 10118 [85, 87, 88, 91].

2.3.4 Authentication Mechanisms

These mechanisms are used to provide the authentication service. An authentication mechanisms consists of a set of rules for exchanging messages between two or more entities. Executing an authentication mechanism must lead to an authentication decision (i.e. whether or not a participating entity is deemed to be authenticated). Such mechanisms are also called 'authentication exchange mechanisms' in ISO 7498-2 [84].

2.3.5 Time-Stamps

A time-stamp can be included in a message to enable its freshness to be verified. To prevent time-stamps being manipulated by active attackers, they must be protected by cryptographic means. Two types of time-stamps are commonly discussed, namely clock-based time-stamps and logical time-stamps (i.e. bilaterally managed sequence numbers). In this thesis, we focus on clock-based time-stamps.

A clock-based time-stamp consists of a time value, typically taken from the clock of the sender of a message. The use of time-stamps in security protocol messages requires all participating entities to be equipped with securely synchronised clocks. Moreover, every entity must define a 'time acceptance window', so that a received message is deemed 'fresh' if and only if its time-stamp falls within this window.

2.3.6   Nonces

A nonce (derived from Number used ONCE) is a value (typically chosen at random) that can be used to establish the freshness of a message sent as part of a challenge-response authentication protocol. A nonce value, as its name indicates, must only be used once within the lifetime of the associated cryptographic key.

2.3.7   Zero-Knowledge Mechanisms

Zero knowledge mechanisms can be used to provide the authentication service. These mechanisms enable an entity to demonstrate knowledge of a secret without revealing it. The zero-knowledge property guarantees that an observer learns nothing about the secret as a result of executing the protocol. Zero-knowledge authentication protocols are standardised in ISO/IEC 9798-5 [92]. Examples of zero-knowledge protocols include the Schnorr protocol [161], and the Feige-Fiat-Shamir identification Scheme [65].

Schnorr Zero-Knowledge Protocol

One of the simplest and most widely discussed zero knowledge protocols is the Schnorr protocol. The security of this protocol rests on the assumption that the Discrete Logarithm Problem[2] is difficult [122]. The goal of the protocol is to enable a prover, P, to prove knowledge of a private authenticator (or secret), $\bar{a}$, to a verifier, V, without revealing the actual value of $\bar{a}$. The operation of the protocol is described below.

---

[2]The Discrete Logarithm Problem is as follows: given an element g in a finite group G and another element $h \in G$, find an integer x such that $g^x = h$. http://www.rsa.com

The protocol requirements are:

1. **Public parameters**: p, q and g, where p and q are large primes satisfying $q|(p-1)$ (where $|$ denotes *factor of*), and g is an element of multiplicative order q in the set of integers modulo p, $\mathbb{Z}_p^*$. These parameters must be made known to both P and V.

2. **Private value**: $\tilde{a}$, $1 \leq \tilde{a} \leq q-1$, chosen by P and kept secret.

3. **Public value**: c, where $c = g^{-\tilde{a}} \bmod p$. This value must be made known to both P and V. It is assumed that it is computationally infeasible to deduce $\tilde{a}$ from c, i.e. we assume that the Discrete Logarithm Problem is difficult with respect to g in $\mathbb{Z}_p^*$.

The protocol operates as follows.

1. P: picks r, where r is a random integer $(1 \leqslant r \leqslant q-1)$.

2. P: sends d to V, where $d = g^r \bmod p$.

3. V: sends a challenge e to P, where e is a random integer $(1 \leqslant e \leqslant 2^t)$.

4. P: sends y to V, where $y = r + e\tilde{a} \bmod q$.

5. V: checks whether or not $d = g^y c^e \bmod p$. If they are equal then P must know the private authenticator $\tilde{a}$, since P could not have computed y successfully without prior knowledge of $\tilde{a}$.

2.4   Security Protocols

2.4.1   Secure Sockets Layer and Transport Layer Security

Netscape[3] originated the Secure Sockets Layer (SSL) protocol, which was first published in 1995 [77]. Version 3.1 of this protocol, adopted by the IETF in 1999 [57], is known as Transport Layer Security (TLS) version 1.0. The latest version of TLS is 1.1 [58].

SSL/TLS is a security protocol designed to provide reliable end-to-end data confidentiality services by applying symmetric encryption mechanisms to the transport layer messages in the TCP/IP protocol stack [26]. For further information on SSL/TLS see, for example, [165, 169].

2.4.2   Security Assertion Markup Language

The Security Assertion Markup Language (SAML) is an XML-based standard for exchanging authentication and/or authorisation information between network entities. The latest version of SAML is SAML 2.0, which is incompatible in many respects with its predecessor SAML 1.1[4].

The most recent version of the SAML specifications (i.e. version 2.0) define three components of an identity management system:

1. Security assertions, that can be used to carry information about the user [40, 120].

---

[3]http://netscape.aol.com/
[4]The main differences between SAML 2.0 and SAML 1.1 are discussed in:
https://spaces.internet2.edu/display/SHIB/SAMLDiffs
and in: http://www.xml.com/pub/a/2005/01/12/saml2.html

2. Profiles and bindings, used for requesting and managing these assertions [37, 82, 121].

3. Metadata, that can employed to describe the offered services [42].

Note that the previous version of the specifications, i.e. SAML 1.1, only defines the first two of these components. Each of the three components listed above builds on the components earlier in the list. Thus security assertions can be used without the protocol profiles and bindings, but not vice versa. Similarly, defining metadata is only meaningful within the context of SAML bindings and protocols.

The SAML 2.0 specifications define two classes of Single Sign-On authentication profiles (or methods), namely the Web Browser profiles (Artifact and POST), and the Enhanced Client or Proxy (ECP) profile [82]. The Liberty profiles described in detail in Section 4.4.1.1 (i.e. Artifact, Browser-POST, and LEC) are very similar to the SAML profiles.

A *SAML assertion*, as defined in [40, 120], can carry three types of security information (or statements):

1. **Authentication statement**: such a statement indicates whether or not the user has been authenticated, and, if so, it specifies the authentication method used (e.g. password) and the time of the authentication.

2. **Attribute statement**: such a statement contains information about the user (e.g. first name, email address, etc.).

3. **Authorization decision statement**: such a statement contains a recommended access control decision (i.e. whether or not the user should be allowed to access a given resource).

SAML assertion requests and responses need to be mapped to communications protocols for transmission; this process is known as *binding*. The most widely discussed binding options are to transmit SAML messages over HTTP or SOAP. SOAP is an XML-based protocol that defines a message container that can used to carry structured information [129]. SOAP messages (or envelopes) can be protected using the WS-Security protocol (described in 2.4.3).

Both the Liberty ID-FF version 1.1 and the Shibboleth version 1.x specifications support SAML 1.1 (where Liberty and Shibboleth are Federated identity management systems, discussed in detail in Chapter 4). However, as a result of a number of operational limitations of the SAML 1.1 protocols, both these schemes employ proprietary protocols. Most of the services supported by the latest versions of the Liberty and Shibboleth specifications (versions 1.2 and 2 respectively) are supported by SAML 2.0; however a few minor incompatibilities between SAML 2.0 and Liberty ID-FF 1.2 remain[5].

2.4.3   Web Services Protocols

Web services are XML-based standards that aim to enable interoperability between software applications running on different platforms [24]. Web services specifications (known collectively as WS-*) define the required means to convert platform oriented applications into web applications that can run on a wide range of platforms.

For the purposes of this thesis, the most important web services are as follows.

- **WS-Security**: defines a standard means to secure SOAP messages using XML-Encryption and XML-Signature [62, 63] (the use of XML Encryption

---

[5]The main differences between SAML 2.0 and ID-FF 1.2 are discussed in:
http://saml.xml.org/differences-between-saml-v2-0-and-liberty-id-ff-1-2
and in: https://spaces.internet2.edu/display/SHIB/SAMLLibertyDiffs

can be omitted if the messages are carried over a secure channel such as is provided by SSL/TLS or IPsec [115]). It also describes how to attach security tokens to SOAP messages [135].

- **WS-Trust**: defines a standard means for exchanging security tokens carried in SOAP messages [134].

- **WS-SecurityPolicy**: defines a standard means for a web service to express its security policy in the form of short messages called policy assertions [133].

- **WS-MetdataExchange**: defines a standard means to retrieve the metadata associated with an endpoint at which a web service is available [54].

- **WS-Addressing**: defines a standard means to exchange the addressing information of a web services application server [25].

2.4.4 Diffie-Hellman Key Exchange

Diffie-Hellman Key Exchange (DHKE) [59] is a cryptographic protocol that enables two entities to jointly establish a shared secret key over an insecure communications channel (i.e. the protocol goals are met even if an attacker can eavesdrop on all the messages exchanged during a protocol run), although the basic form of the protocol does not protect against active attacks. The protocol does not require the communicating entities to have prior knowledge of each other. The established key can subsequently be used with symmetric cryptographic mechanisms.

The protocol requires three public parameters to be established prior to use. These are a generating element, g, in G, where G is finite cyclic group, and a large prime p. It is assumed that these parameters are known by all the entities in the application domain even possible attackers. It is also required that the Discrete Logarithm Problem is difficult with respect to g in G.

If the entities trying to establish a shared secret key are *Alice* and *Bob*, then the protocol operates as follows.

1. **Alice**: picks a random integer, a, and sends $g^a \bmod p$ to **Bob**.

2. **Bob**: picks a random integer, b, and sends $g^b \bmod p$ to **Alice**.

3. **Alice**: computes $(g^b)^a \bmod p$.

4. **Bob**: computes $(g^a)^b \bmod p$.

Alice and Bob now have a shared secret key, $g^{ab} \bmod p$. Even if an eavesdropper, Eve, intercepts all the exchanged message, she cannot compute the value of the secret key.

The DHKE protocol is standardised in RFC 2631 [152], and forms an essential part of many security protocols, including SSL/TLS (see Section 2.4.1).

2.5 Public Key Infrastructures

A *Public Key Infrastructure* (PKI) is made up of a set of services, applications and administrative tools designed to enable the management and distribution of public keys for use with asymmetric cryptographic algorithms.

Within a PKI, a trusted party called a *Certification Authority* (CA) is responsible for certifying identities by issuing their owners with digitally signed public key certificates. These certificates bind a public key to an identity. The most widely used format for such a public key certificate is defined in X.509 [106].

A CA must verify the identity of an applicant for a public key certificate before issuing the certificate. Identity verification procedures vary from one PKI to another;

the level of trustworthiness of a certificate relies on the degree of rigour of this procedure. For further information on PKIs see, for example, [67, 138].

Identity Management

Contents

In this chapter we provide overviews of the notion of identity and of identity management in Sections 3.1 and 3.2, respectively. In section 3.3 we describe a conceptual identity management model as well as a number of practical models. We also cover a number of related topics including Single Sign-On, Level of Assurance, identity source discovery, security policies, proof-of-rightful-possession, and the use of pseudonyms and temporary IDs. Section 3.4 concludes the chapter.

3.1 Identities

The term *Identity* is used here to mean the representation of an entity in a given context, where an *entity* is something that has a distinct existence and can be uniquely identified (e.g. a person or an organisation). This representation takes the form of a defined collection of entity attributes or distinctive characteristics [101]. These attributes and characteristics are also collectively referred to as personally identifiable information (PII).

In line with this use of the term, a recent draft of ITU-T X.1250 [103] defines identity as the *"Representation of an entity (or group of entities) in the form of one or more information elements which allow the entity(s) to be uniquely recognised within a context to the extent that is necessary (for the relevant applications)."*

Whilst, in principle, every entity has a 'whole' identity that consists of all its distinctive attributes, subsets of these attributes can form different 'partial' identities in different contexts. An *identifier* is a unique label for an object, that can be used to refer to an entity in a specific context (e.g. a username that refers to a user's digital account) [101]. We can consider an identifier as a special attribute of an entity that must be unique within its context of use. Figure 3.1 shows the relationship between entities, identities and identifiers. As shown in the figure, an identity is a representation of a subset of all possible attributes of a given entity. Attributes can be shared by different identities of a given entity.

Identification can be defined as a *"process to determine that presented identity information associated with a particular entity is sufficient for the entity to be recognised in a particular domain"* [101]. A representation of an identity in a digital system is called a *digital identity*. Henceforth, 'identity' is used to mean 'digital identity' unless we explicitly state otherwise.

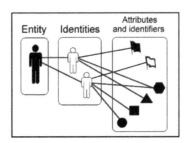

Figure 3.1: Relationship between entities, identities and identifiers

Figure 3.2 shows a possible identity lifecycle which includes five steps, namely: provision, propagate, use, maintain, and deprovision [181]. In the *provision* step, an identity is created by defining an identity record that includes the correct attributes. This step involves identity *registration* to allow an entity to be known within a particular domain of applicability. This requires an initial entity authentication to be performed, i.e. a particular form of authentication based on identity evidence, performing which is a necessary condition for the identity record to be created [101]. This identity record can be propagated to other systems or subsystems (e.g. a database system) in the *propagate* step. After being provisioned and propagated, the identity record can be used by authorised entities in the *use* step. The identity record can be updated and its information can be changed in the *maintain* step, where the identity record must be repropagated after being updated. Finally, the identity record is deleted in the *deprovision* step.

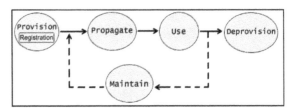

Figure 3.2: Digital identity lifecycle

In 2008, the OECD published a document specifying certain *Properties of Identity*

[3]. These properties apply to 'personal identities' (i.e. identities that belong to individual humans), and for each property the OECD describes how the OECD privacy guidelines (discussed in Section 2.2.7.2) apply to it. We list below these identity properties, along with their OECD descriptions.

1. **Identity is social**. Humans are naturally social, and to engage in social interactions requires that people be able to connect the past to the present, and the present to the future. People need, in other words, something that persists and that can be used as a basis for recognition of persons — an 'identity'.

2. **Identity is subjective**. Different people have different experiences with the same individual and therefore attribute different characteristics to that individual; that is, they will construct different identities for him.

3. **Identity is valuable**. By building a history of a person's past actions, an exchange of identity information creates social capital and enables transactions that would not be possible without identity. In other words, identity lends predictability to afford a comfortable level of confidence for people making decisions.

4. **Identity is referential**. An identity is not a person; it is only a reference to a person.

5. **Identity is composite**. Some information about a person arises from the person himself; he volunteers it. But much information about him is developed by other actors without his involvement.

6. **Identity is consequential**. Because identity tells of a person's past actions, the decision to exchange identity information carries consequences. Disclosure of identity information in a certain context can cause harm; failure to disclose identity information in another context can create risk.

7. **Identity is dynamic**. Identity information is always changing; any particular identity dossier might be inaccurate at any given moment.

8. **Identity is contextual.** People have different identities that they may wish to keep entirely separate. Information can be harmful in the wrong context, or it can simply be irrelevant. Keeping identities separate allows a person to have more autonomy.

9. **Identity is equivocal.** The process of identification is inherently error-prone.

3.2 Identity Management

A recent draft of ITU-T recommendation Y.2720 [102] defines *identity management* as a *"set of functions and capabilities (e.g. administration, management and maintenance, discovery, communication exchanges, correlation and binding, policy enforcement, authentication and assertions) used for*:

- *assurance of identity information (e.g. identifiers, credentials, attributes);*
- *assurance of the identity of an entity (e.g. users/subscribers, groups, user devices, organisations, network and service providers, network elements and objects, and virtual objects); and*
- *enabling business and security applications"*.

A similar definition of identity management can be found in the first committee draft of ISO/IEC 24760 [101]; identity management is defined there as a set of processes, policies and technologies that help authoritative sources as well as individual entities to manage and use identity information. An *authoritative source* (or *identity authority*) of identity information is a place from which a relying party can obtain reliable information about the attributes of a given entity [101].

Identity management processes include: management of the identity lifecycle, management of identity information, and management of entity authentication as a preparatory step for authorisation. Identity management is an essential part of many security services, since it provides assurance of user legitimacy. As a result, identity management is an integral part of any access management system [101].

Since identity management requires storing, processing, and transforming identity information, it raises many privacy concerns. Moreover, requirements for privacy and identity management may conflict. For example, while it is a privacy requirement to minimise the amount of identity information collected about a person (according to the first of the OECD principles for personal data protection discussed in section 2.2.7), this may effect the level of assurance that can be obtained regarding the correctness of the claimed identity of a person. Hence protecting user privacy in identity management systems is a challenging issue [51, 168].

3.3   Identity Management Models

In this section we give a conceptual model for identity management; we then provide an introduction to the concept of Single Sign-On. Finally, we define three categories of identity management systems which cover most of the widely discussed schemes, namely isolated, Information Card-based, and Federated identity management systems.

3.3.1   Conceptual Model

Although a variety of identity management schemes have been proposed, these schemes have similar primary goals and share many technical features. In this thesis, we focus on 'web-based' identity management schemes. Such schemes are of considerable practical significance because of the growing use of web applications.

It has become common, or even necessary, for Internet users to possess multiple digital identities. Managing these identities and protecting the corresponding credentials are difficult problems. This is because of the need for growing numbers of such identities, and the major security threats posed by criminal activities such as identity theft. Web-based identity management aim to address the growing range of security threats and to simplify identity management for both Internet users and service providers.

Web-based identity management systems use the World Wide Web[1] and Web Services (WS) (see section 2.4.3) protocols as the communication means between parties. These schemes have been primarily developed to manage Internet users' digital identities.

Three main parties can be identified within the web-based identity management model:

1. **The Identity Provider or Identity Issuer** (IdP) issues an identity to the user, and is trusted by the other parties for the purposes of identity management. The IdP is essentially an 'identity authority' (see Section 3.2).

2. **The Service Provider** (SP) (or Relying Party (RP) in Microsoft[2] terminology), needs to identify the user before providing services to him/her.

3. **The User** needs to use the SP services. Typically, the user employs a *user agent* (e.g. a web browser) as the means by which she/he interacts with the IdPs and SPs.

---

[1] http://www.w3.org/WWW
[2] http://www.microsoft.com

All web-based identity management systems adhere to the same conceptual model, shown in Figure 3.3. In order for the user to use the services offered by a specific SP, it must first be authenticated by an IdP that is trusted by the target SP. Subsequently, the SP asks the IdP for cryptographically-protected statements (or assertions) about the authenticity and/or attributes of the user. The SP then uses the provided statements to help decide whether or not the user should be permitted to use its services.

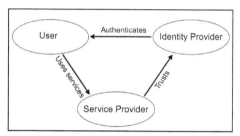

Figure 3.3: An identity management conceptual model

Both the IdP and the SP have their own *security polices*. The IdP security policy includes information specific to individual users, including: how the user should be authenticated, which SPs it can send assertions about that user to, and which user attributes can be asserted. The SP security policy specifies which IdPs it trusts, how users must be authenticated by a specific IdP, and what types of attributes must be asserted by a specific IdP in order for a user to be granted the requested services.

A process called *discovery of identity source* (or simply *discovery*) [101] must take place during the user authentication process. This step enables the system to locate the IdP which is to be asked for an assertion. This step could be performed by either the user machine or the SP server; however, performing it on the user machine has the advantage of giving some protection against phishing attacks. Specifically, if a malicious SP performs discovery, then it could direct the user client to a fake IdP.

If there is a need for direct communication between the IdP and the SP, e.g. in order to exchange information about a user, then, depending on the identity management system in use, they may use a pseudonym or a temporary ID to refer to the user instead of the registered user identity. Such a procedure helps to preserve user anonymity (see Section 2.2.6).

If assertions are passed from the IdP to the SP via the user agent, then some identity management systems allow the user agent to prove its rightful possession of the assertion to the SP. This mitigates the risk of attacks in which an attacker uses an assertion issued to another user to impersonate that user. Such services are known variously as *proof-of-rightful-possession*, *subject confirmation* or *proof-key* methods. A variety of techniques for providing such proof have been proposed, and specific examples are described in Section 3.3.4.2 and 3.3.4.3. Before proceeding we observe that the so-called *Bearer* technique does not provide the SP with any cryptographic evidence that the user who forwarded a security token has the right to possess it. Use of this technique therefore increases this risk of an imposter using a stolen security token to gain access to an SP.

Identity management frameworks can be classified into the following three main classes, depending on the nature of the IdP/IdP and IdP/SP relationships [6].

1. **Isolated framework**. In such a framework there is no co-operation between parties to support user authentication. The SP trusts only itself, and also plays the role of the IdP.

2. **Centralised framework**. A framework of this type has a single IdP that provides identity services to other participating SPs within a closed domain or 'circle of trust'.

3. **Distributed framework**. In such a framework each party within a given group trusts some or all of the parties within this group. This means that

every party within a group is either an IdP that is trusted by some or all members of this group, or an SP that trusts some or all of the IdPs within the group.

In this thesis we are concerned with centralised and distributed identity management frameworks.

3.3.2 Single Sign-on

Single Sign-on (SSO) is an access control feature which allows a user to access multiple SPs during a session, after being authenticated only once by a trusted authentication authority (e.g. an IdP). Obviously, all accessed SPs must trust this authority's decision regarding the legitimacy of the user. A system that supports SSO typically also provides support for 'Single Sign-off' (where a user signs-off just once and is then automatically signed-off from all accessed SPs).

One important property of SSO, as we define it, is that it must work without the need for the user to participate interactively (in real time) in the authentication process, or in any other identification relevant process, more than once in a single working session. That is the SSO feature should work transparently to the user, since one of the main reasons for deploying an SSO system is user convenience.

Although SSO potentially enhances both system usability and user convenience, its use also raises significant security concerns. This is because, in many SSO systems, if an attacker breaks the authentication process with the authentication authority (e.g. by cracking the user password) then she/he can readily access all the participating SPs [71].

3.3.3 Level of Assurance

A widely used definition of the term *Level of Assurance* (LoA) in the context of identity management, states [23] that LoA is:

1. the degree of confidence in the vetting process used to establish the identity of the individual to whom the credential was issued (i.e. the degree of confidence in the registration process); and

2. the degree of confidence that the individual who uses the credential is the individual to whom the credential was issued (i.e. the degree of confidence in the authentication process).

The concept of LoA is also referred to in the literature as Personal Identity Verification (PIV) Authentication Level, PIV Assurance Level, Identity Assurance Level, Authentication Profile, Authentication Context, and Authentication Assurance Level.

It is clear that an SP's level of assurance that a user is truly who he/she claims to be depends on both the authentication process used by the IdP and the IdP's initial identity registration process [47]. Accordingly, an SP could define an access control system that gives the same user different access rights and privileges depending on the SP's level of confidence in the IdP's registration and authentication processes.

In 2006, the US National Institute of Standards and Technology[3] (NIST) published its *Electronic Authentication Guideline* [29], which adopted Office of Management and Budget[4] (OMB) guidance originally published in 2003 under the title *E-Authentication Guidance for Federal Agencies* [23]. According to these two documents, LoA can be classified into 4 levels, where Level 1 is lowest and 4 is highest.

The main features of the OMB/NIST levels are as follows.

- **Level 1**: This level does not require any proof of identity during the registration process. However, it provides a range of methods to be used in the
  authentication process. Although a simple username/password authentication
  method is permitted at this level, plaintext passwords must not be transmitted
  across a network. However, this level does not require the use of cryptographic
  methods that block offline attacks by an eavesdropper. At Level 1, long-term
  shared authentication secrets may be revealed to verifiers. Assertions issued
  about users as a result of a successful authentication by the IdP must be either
  cryptographically authenticated by the SP or obtained directly from the IdP
  via a secure authentication protocol.

- **Level 2**: This level mandates a single factor authentication process. At Level
  2, identity proof requirements are introduced, requiring presentation of identifying materials or information during the registration process. Eavesdropper,
  replay, and on-line guessing attacks are prevented. Long-term shared authentication secrets, if used, are never revealed to any party except the claimant
  and verifiers operated by the Credentials Service Provider (CSP); however,
  session (temporary) shared secrets may be provided to independent verifiers
  by the CSP. Assertions issued about users as a result of a successful authentication by the IdP must be either cryptographically authenticated by the SP
  or obtained directly from the IdP via a secure authentication protocol.

- **Level 3**: This level mandates a multi-factor authentication process. A minimum of two authentication factors is required. At this level, identity proof
  procedures require verification of identifying materials and information. Level
  3 authentication is based on 'proof of possession' of a key or a 'one-time password' through a cryptographic protocol. Level 3 authentication requires the

---

[3]http://www.nist.gov
[4]http://www.whitehouse.gov/omb

use of cryptographically strong mechanisms to protect the primary authentication token (secret key, private key or one-time password) against compromise by protocol threats including: eavesdropper, replay, on-line guessing, verifier impersonation and man-in-the-middle attacks. Long-term shared authentication secrets, if used, are never revealed to any party except the claimant and verifiers operated directly by the Credentials Service Provider (CSP); however, session (temporary) shared secrets may be provided to independent verifiers by the CSP. Approved cryptographic techniques are used for all operations. Assertions issued about users as a result of a successful authentication by the IdP must be either cryptographically authenticated by the SP or obtained directly from the IdP via a secure authentication protocol.

- **Level 4**: This level is intended to provide the highest practical authentication assurance. Level 4 authentication is based on proof of possession of a key through a cryptographic protocol. The user token shall be a hardware cryptographic module validated at FIPS 140-2 Level 2 [140] or higher, with at least FIPS 140-2 Level 3 physical security. By requiring a physical token which cannot readily be copied, and since FIPS 140-2 requires operator authentication at Level 2 and higher, this level ensures robust, two-factor, remote authentication. Eavesdropper, replay, on-line guessing, verifier impersonation and man-in-the-middle attacks are prevented. Long-term shared authentication secrets, if used, are never revealed to any party except the claimant and verifiers operated directly by the Credentials Service Provider (CSP); however, session (temporary) shared secrets may be provided to independent verifiers by the CSP. All sensitive data transfers are cryptographically authenticated using keys bound to the authentication process.

In 2007, the Interoperable Delivery of European eGovernment Services to Public Administrations, Businesses and Citizens[5] organisation (IDABC) published a document entitled '*Proposal for a multi-level authentication mechanism and a mapping*

66

of existing authentication mechanisms' [73], in which four levels of assurance are proposed: minimal assurance, low assurance, substantial assurance, and high assurance. These levels are similar to the OMB/NIST levels, and cover both registration and authentication processes.

It would potentially be helpful if the concept of LoA could be integrated into the currently used assertion exchange protocols (e.g. SAML), so that the IdP could specify the LoA of every assertion it provides. According to a survey conducted by the Joint Information Systems Committee[6] (JISC) [109], 83% of surveyed IdPs would be willing to follow technical guidance on the use of LoA if such guidance was available. Fortunately, SAML 2.0 provides the means to express the LoA of assertions [114, 171]. A recent European Network and Information Security Agency[7] (ENISA) report [4] proposes a model for mapping the IDABC levels to SAML 2.0.

Both the OMB/NIST and the IDABC levels have been criticised for the fact that they focus only on the user authentication process, and do not cover user identity attributes (as used for authorisation) [47]. Moreover, even though the OMB/NIST and IDABC LoA metrics combine the registration and the authentication processes, Chadwick [47] suggests that *"it is more useful if the LOA is split into two separate metrics, one for registration of the identity attributes, and one for the authentication method being used in the current session"*. A further limitation of the OMB/NIST and IDABC levels of assurance is that they combine both symmetric and asymmetric cryptography within the same level, which can be confusing for implementers [146].

---

[5]http://ec.europa.eu/idabc
[6]http://www.jisc.ac.uk
[7]http://www.enisa.europa.eu

3.3.4 Practical Models

In this section we describe three categories of identity management systems which cover most widely discussed schemes. These categories are defined in terms of the techniques used for user authentication and identification. We refer to these three categories as *practical models* (as distinct from the conceptual models introduced in Section 3.3.1).

3.3.4.1 Isolated Identity Management

An *isolated* identity management scheme is one in which there is no cooperation between parties for the purposes of user authentication [111]. Historically, most Internet service providers operated isolated identity management systems. As a result, users were, and often still are, required to maintain a distinct identifier for each service provider. As shown in figure 3.4, in the isolated model the service provider is also an identity provider (i.e. the service provider issues identities to its users).

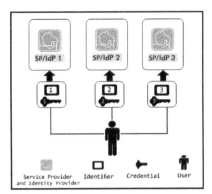

Figure 3.4: Isolated identity management model

Isolated identity management schemes are primarily designed to aid service providers rather than the end users. For example, many service providers deploy automated systems to manage digital identities; however, these systems do not help end users, who must manage their digital identities manually.

In many isolated identity management systems, service providers authenticate users using an application layer technique (e.g. username and password), whereas user agents (e.g. web browsers) authenticate service providers using a lower layer technique (such as SSL/TLS). Managing multiple digital identities and protecting the associated credentials in such an environment can become very difficult for users.

3.3.4.2   Information Card-based Identity Management

An *Information Card-based* identity management (ICIM) scheme (also known as a claim-based identity management scheme [20, 123]) is one which has the following properties:

- for each IdP with which the user has a relationship, there is a defined set of claims, i.e. pieces of PII for which the IdP is prepared to generate an assertion;
- when using the system, the user is presented with a choice of IdPs using a 'card-based' user interface;
- at least one proof-of-rightful-possession method is supported (see Section 3.3.1);
- users are capable of asserting their own claims; and
- IdP discovery is performed on the user machine.

ICIM schemes have been designed to make identity management easier for Internet users; such schemes enable users to employ their IdP-asserted PII to identify themselves to SPs, instead of using service provider specific identifiers (e.g. usernames) and access credentials (e.g. passwords).

In order to authenticate a user, the SP can request a 'security token' containing assertions of the values of certain pieces of user PII (i.e. claims). This security token must be signed by an IdP trusted by the SP. The user agent obtains a security token from an IdP, after being authenticated, and forwards it to the SP.

As stated above, ICIM schemes make use of virtual *Information Cards* (also referred to as InfoCards, or i-Cards), where IdPs issue such cards to users (typically in the form of XML files). Information Cards are stored on user machines, and hold (relatively) non-sensitive meta-information related to the user, including the types of claim that can be asserted (if required by the target SP), and information about the IdP that issued it (Chapter 4 provides more details on the contents of Information Cards used by specific examples of ICIM systems). During use, a user chooses one of the Information Cards stored on her/his machine to identify themselves to the SP that they wish to access. An IdP is able to assert the values of any claims listed in an Information Card it has issued. This is somewhat similar to the identification process we experience in real life, where we use physical ID cards (issued by a trusted authority) that have information about us stored in it and/or printed on it (e.g. a personal photo) in order to identify ourselves. Figure 3.5 shows the inter-entity relationships in the ICIM model.

In an ICIM system, an enabling component known as the *Identity Selector* [125] needs to be present on the user machine. This component performs several important tasks including: providing a user-friendly interface for Information Card management and security token viewing, negotiating the security requirements of the SPs and IdPs, supporting identity provider discovery, controlling and managing user authentication to the IdP, and generating self-issued security tokens. Self-issued tokens contain assertions made by the users about themselves, and are generated by the Self-issued Identity Provider (SIP), part of the Identity Selector.

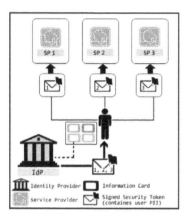

Figure 3.5: Information Card-based identity management model

Identity provider discovery in ICIM systems is performed by the user in conjunction with the user agent and the Identity Selector. The Identity Selector prompts the user to choose one of the Information Cards that support the claims which the target SP wishes to have asserted. By choosing an Information Card the user implicitly selects the IdP that will be asked for a security token, since Information Cards are specific to IdPs. We describe in greater detail how IdP discovery is performed in specific examples of ICIM systems in Chapter 4.

In an ICIM system, the user is authenticated by the IdP through the Identity Selector. A user is required to present her security credentials to the Identity Selector (e.g. a username/password) so they can be passed to the IdP before it issues the requested security token. This authentication step must be performed every time before a security token can be issued, even if the user chooses to use the same InfoCard/IdP to access multiple SPs[8]. This means that an ICIM system cannot offer an SSO service, following the definition of the term given in Section 3.3.2.

---

[8]This has been verified by experiment for the CardSpace ICIM.

71

Each Information Card typically has a global unique ID, and this ID can be used by the IdP to generate a new 'secret' long-term SP-specific ID (usually referred to as the *Private Personal Identifier* (PPID)) [137]. In the case of a self-issued Information Card, the SIP will generate the PPID. This PPID must be registered with the SP, and is known only by the IdP (or the SIP) and the SP; even the user cannot obtain a full PPID from the Identity Selector. PPIDs act as pseudonyms (see Section 2.2.6), and are used for identification purposes, e.g. by requesting the Identity Selector to obtain a security token from the IdP (or the SIP) that contains a specific PPID. Both types of ID, i.e. the global Information Card ID and the PPID, are treated as user claims.

A common feature of ICIM systems is that their identity management framework can be used for both authentication and authorisation. This is possible because the ICIM model allows SPs to request signed assertions of unique identifiers as well as other user attributes (they are all considered as claims).

ICIM systems typically offer three 'proof-of-rightful-possession' methods [125]:

1. *Symmetric*. In this method, the Identity Selector must reveal to the IdP the identity of the SP to which the user is trying to log-in. The IdP generates a secret key, encrypts it with the SP's public key, and inserts it into the security token. This secret key is also sent directly to the Identity Selector (over an SSL/TLS channel) in a separate message. The Identity Selector can now use this secret key to prove rightful possession of the security token to the SP (e.g. by decrypting or MACing specific data using the secret key), since only the legitimate holder of the security token possesses the secret key.

2. *Asymmetric*. In this method, the Identity Selector generates an ephemeral RSA key pair, and sends the public key to the IdP. The IdP inserts this public key into the security token. The Identity Selector can then use the

corresponding private key to prove rightful possession of the security token to the SP (e.g. by signing specific data using the private key).

3. *Bearer.* As noted in Section 3.3.1, use of this method does not provide the SP with any cryptographic evidence that the user who forwarded a security token has the right to possess it. This means that the SP must assume that any user who provides a security token is the rightful owner. This method increases this risk of an imposter using a stolen security token to gain access to an SP.

The *Security Token Service* (STS) is a component of an ICIM system responsible for security policy and token management at the IdP and, optionally, at the SP [108].

The most widely discussed example of an ICIM system is Microsoft CardSpace[9]. Other ICIM systems include OpenInfoCard[10], Higgins[11], and DigitalMe[12]. DigitalMe is supported by the Bandit Project[13]. In this thesis we focus on Microsoft CardSpace because of its ubiquity as part of Windows Vista and Windows 7; however, many of the observations made in the remainder of this thesis regarding Microsoft CardSpace also apply to other ICIM systems since they have strong similarities to one another.

Finally we observe that, since they cannot provide SSO (as discussed above), ICIM systems do not adopt the SAML SSO profiles (see Section 2.4.2). For further details see Chapter 4.

---

[9]http://www.microsoft.com/net/cardspace.aspx
[10]http://code.google.com/p/openinfocard
[11]http://www.eclipse.org/higgins
[12]More implementations are listed at: http://www.osis.idcommons.net
[13]http://bandit-project.org

3.3.4.3 Federated Identity Management

A *Federated* identity management (FIM) scheme is one which has the following properties:

- identity federation process is supported, in which the user SP-issued identity is linked with the user IdP-issued identity;
- the use of public global identifiers is not supported (as discussed below);
- SSO is supported;
- the scheme is built on an open, standardised, communication framework (e.g. the SAML SSO profiles); and
- at least one proof-of-rightful-possession method is supported.

In a Federated identity management system, the user might have one or more 'local' identities issued by SPs, in addition to a single identity issued by the IdP within a specific domain called a *circle of trust* (CoT). A typical CoT consists of a single IdP and multiple SPs. The IdPs of a CoT must be trusted by all the SPs within it. An SP can be a member of more that one CoT. A user can federate her/his IdP-issued identity with the local identities issued by SPs within the same CoT [101, 181].

Federating two identifies (where they exist) means linking them together so that if a user has been successfully authenticated as the holder of one (e.g. the IdP-issued identity), then he/she will be automatically deemed as the holder of the others, without the need for another authentication process in the same working session. This linking process is called *identity federation*. The process of identity federation has to be initiated by an SP; typically, when a user logs-in to an SP, the SP will check if that user has an IdP-issued identity. If so, then the SP can offer the user the opportunity to federate his/her local identity with his/her IdP-issued identity.

Federating identities requires the user to separately authenticate to the SP and the IdP. If the user has federated several IdPs with an SP, then it is up to the SP to choose an IdP from amongst them, except in the enabled-client SSO profile (described in Section 4.4.1.1) in which the user can be provided with a list of IdPs to choose from.

In order to support the above federation process, there must be a reliable means for an SP to discover whether or not the user has an IdP-issued identity. This can be achieved by using the 'common domain cookie' technique [82]. This technique involves establishing a CoT-specific common web domain to which every member of that CoT has access, in order for any member to be able to read cookies written by any other member. This would typically involve each member of the CoT owning its own web page under that domain.

For example, suppose that a CoT, *isgCoT* say, includes an IdP, X say, and two SPs, SP_1 and SP_2. The members of this CoT establish a common domain (isg-CoT.com) say, and each member is assigned a sub-domain (e.g. IdPX.isgCoT.com, SP1.isgCoT.com, and SP2.isgCoT.com). The IdP X can then write a cookie from the domain IdPX.isgCoT.com that says, for example, '*I am IdP X, and I have issued an identity to this user*', and store this cookie on the machine of every user it has successfully authenticated (note that the identifier of the IdP-issued identity will never be revealed). Such a cookie is known as a *common domain cookie* (CDC). Subsequently, when a user that has already been authenticated by IdP X logs-in to SP_1 or SP_2, the service provider can read the CDC stored on the user's machine by redirecting the user agent to the service provider sub-domain. If the SP finds an entry from IdP X in the CDC, then they can assume that this user has an IdP-issued identity.

Once federation has taken place for a user's identities, an SP will know which IdP(s) it can ask to supply a token. The SP redirects the user agent (e.g. a web browser) to the relevant IdP. If the user has not already been authenticated during this working session, the IdP authenticates her/him, and redirects the user agent back to the SP with a signed assertion of the fact that this user has been successfully authenticated by the IdP using a specific method at a given time. Finally, the SP checks the information included within the assertion and verifies the IdP's signature; if the SP accepts the assertion, the user will be logged-in to the SP without the need for another authentication procedure. Figure 3.6 shows the inter-entity relationships in the Federated identity management model.

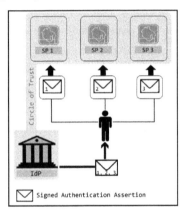

Figure 3.6: Federated identity management model

Typically, an IdP will only authenticate the user once during a single working session. Hence, almost all Federated identity management systems provide support for SSO functionality. Moreover, we observe that most of the Federated identity management systems are built on SAML SSO profiles (see Section 2.4.2).

Unique user identifiers make up a P3P data category that must be protected in order to preserve user privacy (See section 2.2.7). Hence, these identifiers (either local or IdP-issued) must not be shared between CoT members. However, without sharing unique identifiers, it would be difficult to federate two identities belonging to the same user, since the SP and the IdP need to make sure that they are referring to a particular user in the system when they communicate. Typically, a federated identity management system solves this dilemma by using pseudonyms (see Section 2.2.6) instead of the user's pre-issued identifiers, thereby providing unlinkability. The IdP and the SP must agree on specific pseudonyms (also known as *opaque handles*) as references to a particular user during the federation process; this agreement is an important part of what is known as a *federation agreement* procedure. The SAML Persistent ID (PID) field can be used to hold such a pseudonym in an SAML message. The PID is used for essentially the same purpose as the PPID described in Section 3.3.4.2.

As shown in Figure 3.7, the IdP and the SP may agree to use the same pseudonym to refer to a particular user, or they may use distinct pseudonyms. Regardless of how pseudonyms are used, it is clearly important that each party knows which pseudonym the other party will use to refer to a given user. For example, suppose that a user named *Alice* has three identities, an IdP-issued identity, *Alice@IdP*, and two local identities, *Alice.1@SP1* and *Alice.2@SP2*, issued by, SP_1 and SP_2, respectively. The IdP could use one pseudonym (xxx, say) to refer to *Alice* when it communicates with SP_1, and a different pseudonym (yyy, say) when it communicates with SP_2. However, although the IdP is using the pseudonym yyy to refer to *Alice* when it communicates with SP_2, SP_2 may use a different pseudonym ($y123$, say) to refer to the same user when it communicates with the IdP.

However, in some Federated identity management systems, the IdP and the SP do not agree on long-term pseudonyms for a particular user. Instead of using pseudonyms, the IdP and the SP use temporary IDs agreed during the authentication process. Such temporary IDs are typically only used for one working session

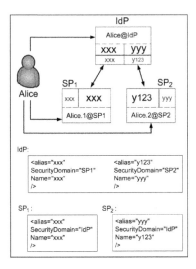

Figure 3.7: Pseudonyms in Federated identity management.

(the use of temporary IDs is discussed in more detail in Chapter 4 in the context of specific examples of FIM systems). Of course the discovery method described above will not work in this case, because no federation process has taken place prior to the user log-in attempt. Therefore, another 'intermediary' discovery method is used, known as 'Where Are You From' (WAYF). In this approach, the user is given a list of IdPs, and must select the IdP that issued the identity to be federated with the user's local identity. Although the user selects the IdP, the discovery is performed by the SP server (i.e. the SP redirects the user to the IdP, after it discovers the target IdP). More details on the WAYF method can be found in [180].

Since most Federated identity management systems rely on the SAML SSO profiles, the IdP and SP can communicate directly by redirecting the user agent from one party to the other, assuming they use the SAML Web Browser profiles (see Section 2.4.2). In this case, no enabling component needs to be installed on the user machine. However, if they use the SAML Enhanced Client profile, then an enabling component is required. These profiles are described in greater detail in Chapter 4.

Federated identity management systems typically offer three 'proof-of-rightful-possession' methods [130, 159]:

1. *Holder-of-Key* (HoK). This method enables the user agent to prove its rightful possession of a specific assertion using a cryptographic key (either symmetric or asymmetric). If a symmetric key is used, then this key must be included in the signed assertion generated by the IdP, after being shared with the user. If an asymmetric private key is used, then the corresponding public key must be included in the signed assertion. How the IdP shares the symmetric secret key or the asymmetric public key with the user agent is usually left to the system implementers. Moreover, if a symmetric key is used, and unlike the ICIM 'symmetric' method, the IdP is not required to encrypt the symmetric (secret) key using the SP's public key. Of course this does not necessarily mean that the key is sent in the clear; it is typically sent over a secure channel (e.g. as provided by SSL/TLS or IPSec).

2. *Sender-Vouches*. This method is only used if the entity that presents the assertion to the SP is not the subject of the assertion, but nevertheless has the permission of the subject to present it to the SP on its behalf. Such an entity is called an *attesting entity*, and must have an existing trust relationship with the SP. The *subject* of an assertion is the party whose attributes are asserted by the IdP-issued assertion. The subject could be an end user or another SP. The attesting entity must sign the assertion (even though it is already signed by the IdP) before forwarding it to the SP.

3. *Bearer*. This method is identical to the ICIM 'bearer' method described in Section 3.3.4.2 above.

These methods are known as the SAML proof-of-rightful-possession (or subject confirmation) methods, since they were first specified in the SAML specifications. Federated identity management systems typically rely on SAML assertions to hold the proof-of-rightful-possession data.

The Liberty Alliance Project[14] scheme is an example of a federated identity management system. Many of the observations we make in this thesis regarding the Liberty Alliance Project system also apply to other Federated identity management systems, since they have strong similarities to one another. Other examples of Federated identity management systems include the SAML 2.0 Federation Framework [40], WS-Federation [136], and Shibboleth[15].

Although the OpenID[16] model is quite similar to the Federated identity management model, OpenID is not a Federated identity management system under the definition used in this thesis. This is because of the lack of explicit trust relationships in the OpenID model, the lack of 'federation' support, and the fact that OpenID does not support any proof-of-rightful-possession method. Further details of OpenID in Chapter 4.

Finally, we observe that the concept of *User-centric identity management* [6, 27, 101, 111, 112] has been proposed as a means of easing the user task of managing digital identities by providing them with more control over their identities. A user-centric identity management system is one that is developed primarily from the perspective of end-users, enabling a user to maintain control over how user PII is created and used, thereby enhancing user privacy. Many identity management systems have been referred to as user-centric, including ICIM systems such as Microsoft CardSpace and PRIME [32], and Federated identity management systems such as UFed [166].

---

[14]http://www.projectliberty.org
[15]http://shibboleth.internet2.edu
[16]http://openid.net

3.4 Conclusions

In this chapter we have provided an overview of the notion of identity. Definitions of identity have been provided, along with a brief description of the identity lifecycle. We have also provided definitions of identity management and related terms such as authoritative source and identity authority.

A web-based conceptual model of identity management has been presented, as well as introductions to SSO systems and the concept of LoA. Finally, descriptions of three practical models of identity management systems have been provided, namely Isolated, Information Card-based, and Federated identity management. The Isolated model is related to the Isolated class discussed in Section 3.3.1, whereas the ICIM and FIM models can be either Centralised or Distributed.

Although the FIM and ICIM models share a number of the properties, as discussed in 3.3.4.2 and 3.3.4.3, each model has its own distinct properties. The FIM model does not support two of the ICIM model properties, namely the possession of a card-based interface, and support for users to assert their own claims[17]. On the other hand, the ICIM model does not support two of the FIM model properties, namely federation and SSO support.

Table 3.1 provides a comparison between Information Card-based and Federated identity management schemes.

---

[17]Many FIM systems support the LEC profile, in which IdP discovery is performed on the user machine.

Table 3.1: Information Card-based versus Federated identity management.

Comparison Point	ICIM	FIM
Discovery of IdP	Performed on the user machine	Typically performed on the SP server
Pseudonyms	Used	Used
Identity federation	Not supported	Supported
Software enabling component on the user machine	Required	Typically not required
Self-issued assertions	Supported	Not supported
Single Sign-On	Not supported	Typically supported
Built on SAML SSO profiles	No	Yes
The IdP must be informed of all the accessed SPs	No	Yes
Proof-of-rightful-possession methods	Symmetric, Asymmetric, and Bearer	Holder-of-Key (Symmetric and Asymmetric), Sender-Vouches, and Bearer

Identity Management Systems

Contents

In this chapter we provide an overview of five of the most widely discussed web-based identity management systems, namely Microsoft CardSpace, the Higgins project, the Liberty Alliance project, the Shibboleth project, and OpenID. These systems are discussed in Sections 4.2, 4.3, 4.4, 4.5, and 4.6, respectively. We also investigate certain security limitations shared by all these systems in Section 4.7.

In Section 4.8 we discuss the practicality of identity management systems, and consider how their practicality can be enhanced by developing reliable integration and delegation schemes. We also provide overviews of the Project Concordia integration framework, and the Shibboleth and OAuth delegation frameworks, as well as reviewing the related literature.

4.1   Introduction

An *identity management system* enables authoritative sources to perform identity management tasks (as described in section 3.2) via an operational framework. Most of today's web-based identity management systems adhere to one of the practical identity management models described in Chapter 3 (i.e. the isolated, Information Card-based or Federated identity management models).

The last few years have seen the development of a number of web-based identity management systems, including AOL OpenAuth[1], Yahoo BBAuth[2], and Flickr Au-

---

[1]http://dev.aol.com/api/openauth
[2]http://developer.yahoo.com/auth

thentication API[3]. Many of these systems are isolated, and they are largely not interoperable with one another.

After an open dialogue with a number of identity management experts, in 2005 Microsoft published its Laws of Identity [33]. These laws reflects Microsoft's vision of the requirements that should be met by any web-based identity management system. A list of these laws, with Microsoft's interpretation of them, is given below (note that we have changed the terminology slightly to use the term 'identity management system' instead of 'identity system').

1. **User control and consent:** The identity management system must only reveal information identifying a user with the user's consent.

2. **Minimal disclosure for a constrained use:** The solution which discloses the least amount of identifying information and best limits its use is the most stable long term solution.

3. **Justifiable parties:** The identity management system must be designed so that the disclosure of identifying information is limited to parties having a necessary and justifiable place in a given identity relationship.

4. **Directed identity:** The identity management system must support both 'omnidirectional' identifiers for use by public entities and 'unidirectional' identifiers for use by private entities.

5. **Pluralism of operators and technologies:** The identity management system must channel and enable the inter-working of multiple identity technologies run by multiple identity providers.

6. **Human integration:** The identity management system must define the human user to be a component of the distributed system, integrated through unambiguous human-machine communication mechanisms offering protection

---

[3]http://www.flickr.com/services/api/misc.userauth.html

against identity attacks.

7. **Consistent experience across contexts:** The identity management system must guarantee its users a simple, consistent experience while enabling separation of contexts through multiple operators and technologies.

It seems reasonable to believe that, by following the laws stated above, identity management systems can reach an acceptable level of usability, reliability, flexibility, and privacy. We also observe that a number of these laws were derived from the OECD principles for personal data protection (see Section 2.2.7). The requirements of Law 1 are covered by principles 6 and 7. Similarly, the requirements of Law 2 are covered by principles 1, 2 and 4, and the requirements of Law 3 are covered by principles 1 and 3.

In this chapter we describe five identity management systems and frameworks, namely Microsoft CardSpace, Higgins, the Liberty Alliance Project, Shibboleth, and OpendID. We also discuss enhancing the practicality of identity management systems by enhancing both their interoperablity (using integration schemes) and their usability and flexibility (using delegation schemes).

4.2 Microsoft CardSpace

Back in 1999, Microsoft introduced .NET Passport, a ticket-based single sign-on system. Although .NET Passport was supported by a number of well-known service providers, such as eBay and Visa, it was not widely used for SSO. The single sign-on features have since been restricted to Microsoft web sites only, and Passport now functions simply as a means of logging-in to these web sites. In 2005, Microsoft published two white papers that discuss the 'failure' of .NET Passport [33, 123], and this analysis has clearly influenced Microsoft's subsequent offerings in this area,

86

including the development of Microsoft CardSpace.

Microsoft CardSpace (henceforth abbreviated to CardSpace) is the name for a Microsoft WinFX software component that is described by Microsoft as an 'identity metasystem'; using our terminology, it is an identity management system. It is designed to comply with the seven Laws of Identity, as promulgated by Microsoft (see Section 4.1). A new version of CardSpace, CardSpace 2.0, is expected to be officially released in 2010 (a Beta version has recently been released); however, Microsoft has stated that it will be compatible with the currently deployed version of CardSpace[4].

4.2.1 The CardSpace Framework

CardSpace provides a way to represent identities using claims, and a means to bridge technology and organisational boundaries using claims transformations [124]. It is an ICIM system, and hence, as discussed in Section 3.3.4.2, is not an SSO system. It aims to reduce the reliance on passwords for Internet user authentication by service providers, and to improve the privacy of personal information.

The CardSpace identity management architecture is designed to provide the user with control over his/her digital identities in a user friendly manner, and to tackle identity management security problems, such as breaches of privacy and identity theft, with no single identity authority control. CardSpace works with Internet Explorer browsers (CardSpace plug-ins for browsers other than Microsoft Internet Explorer have also been developed, such as the Firefox Plug-in[5]).

Digital identities in CardSpace are represented as claims made by one digital subject (e.g. an Internet user) about itself or another digital subject. A claim is an assertion

---

[4]http://technet.microsoft.com/en-us/library/dd996657(WS.10).aspx
[5]https://addons.mozilla.org/en-US/firefox/addon/51667

that certain identifying information (e.g. given name, social security number, credit card number, etc.) belongs to a given digital subject (or entity) [34, 124]. As in any ICIM system (see Section 3.3.4.2), user identifiers (e.g. a username) and attributes (e.g. user gender) are both treated as claims.

As in any ICIM system (see Section 3.3.4.2), The framework is based on the identification process we experience in the real world using physical ID cards. An IdP issues its users with virtual cards called Information Cards (InfoCards); such InfoCards are called *managed cards*. InfoCards can also be self-issued by the users themselves via the SIP (see Section 3.3.4.2), and such InfoCards are known as *personal cards*, or *self-issued cards*. Infocards are stored on the user machine as XML files with the extension '*.crd'. If the InfoCard is self-issued, then the values of the supported claims are stored in encrypted form by the SIP on the user machine.

A managed InfoCard is signed by the issuing IdP. An InfoCard (managed or self-issued) contains the following (relatively) non-sensitive meta-information:

- The image of the card that the user sees on his/her screen.
- The name of the card.
- A Uniform Resource Identifier (URI) [19] from which the issuing IdP's policy can be obtained (managed cards only).
- One or more URIs which can be used to request security tokens from the IdP (managed cards only). For each URI the InfoCard must specify the authentication method that is used by the IdP as a prerequisite to supplying a token. If the authentication method is username/password, then the InfoCard must also contain the username.
- A list of the supported claims that can be asserted by the IdP (or the SIP). This allows the Identity Selector to match an SP's security policy to IdPs that

are able to create security tokens meeting the SP requirements. Self-issued InfoCards can only contain 14 claim types, namely *First Name, Last Name, Email Address, Street, City, State, Postal Code, Country/Region, Home Phone, Other Phone, Mobile Phone, Date of Birth, Gender,* and *Web Page.*

- The types of security tokens that can be requested from this IdP (e.g. a SAML 2.0 assertion). These tokens will contain asserted claims, and must be encapsulated in a WS-Trust message (see Section 2.4.3) and signed by the IdP. The only token type supported for a self-issued InfoCard is a SAML 1.1 assertion.

- The InfoCard creation and expiry times.

- The InfoCard's CardSpace reference, which is a globally unique URI (unique to the IdP). This identifier is created by the issuer IdP (or the SIP in the case of a self-issued InfoCard), and must be passed back to the IdP every time a security token is requested using this InfoCard.

- A flag to indicate whether or not the token requests must include information identifying the SP for which the token will be issued.

- An optional pointer to the privacy policy of the IdP.

When a user tries to log-in to an SP, the SP declares its security policy to the Identity Selector. The SP security policy can be retrieved using the WS-MetadataExchange protocol, and is expressed using the WS-SecurityPolicy and WS-Trust protocols (see Section 2.4.3). The policy includes a variety of information, the most significant elements of which are as follows [47].

- **The issuer**: this field contains the WS-Addressing (see Section 2.4.3) Endpoint References (URIs) of the IdPs that the SP trusts to issue the requested token (e.g. https://isg.rhul.ac.uk/idp). If this field is left blank, then the SP will accept a token from any IdP. If the SP is prepared to accept a self-issued token, then this field must contain the URI 'http://schemas.xmlsoap.org/ws/2005/05/identity/issuer/self'.

- **The claims that must be asserted**: this field contains a list of the claims to be asserted by the IdP. Each claim is flagged as mandatory or optional.

- **The security token type**: this field contains the security token type that the SP will accept (e.g. a SAML assertion). It is important to note that CardSpace identity metasystem itself does not restrict the type of security tokens, i.e. all types of token can be used within the framework as long as they are encapsulated in a WS-Trust message. As previously noted, in the case of a self-issued InfoCard, the only supported token type is a SAML 1.1 assertion.

- **The proof-of-rightful-possession method**: asymmetric, symmetric, or bearer (see Section 3.3.4.2).

The SP security policy can also specify other constraints on the security token (e.g. the maximum token age).

After processing the SP policy, the Identity Selector checks which InfoCards satisfy it and prompts the user to select one of them. Once an InfoCard has been selected, the Identity Selector retrieves the appropriate IdP security policy from the IdP. This policy is specified using WSDL [50], and indicates the protocol messages that must be used to access the IdP-STS. The policy also contains details of how a security token must be retrieved from the IdP, and specifies the security measures that should be applied to the request token (e.g. whether the security token should be encrypted by the IdP using a short-term symmetric session key, or if the encryption provided by SSL/TLS is sufficient) [47]. Additionally, the IdP security policy must contain the IdP's X.509 public key certificate (see Section 2.5).

The identity selector then requests the security token from the issuer IdP. After receiving the request, and prior to authenticating the user and generating the token, the IdP checks what claims it can assert for this user, whether its policy permits it to generate the requested security token, and how the user must be authenticated. If the IdP decides that it can generate the requested token, then it authenticates the user via the Identity Selector interface using the authentication method specified in the policy. Four authentication methods are supported, namely username/password, Kerberos V5 ticket, X.509 certificate (either software-based or using a smart card), and self-issued SAML 1.1 assertion [137].

On receipt of the token from the IdP, the Identity Selector optionally shows its contents to the user; the displayed information is deleted from the system after the user has given consent to proceed. Finally, the Identity Selector forwards the security token to the SP, which will deem the user authenticated if the received token is valid and meets its requirements. Observe that, unlike the PID, in the case where the target scope information is present in the RST, the PPID must be handed to the IdP by the Identity Selector (within the RST), before the IdP can include it in the security token.

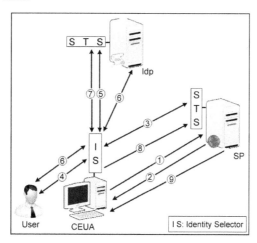

Figure 4.1: CardSpace Framework.

Figure 4.1 provides a simplified sketch of the CardSpace framework. In the figure it is assumed that the user has already been issued an InfoCard by an IdP, and has retrieved the SP web page that offers a CardSpace-based log-in. In step 1, the user clicks on the CardSpace icon in the SP web page using a CardSpace-Enabled User Agent (CEUA), also known as the *Service Requester*, which is essentially a CardSpace-enabled web browser. In step 2, the SP identifies itself using a public key certificate (e.g. a certificate used for SSL/TLS), and triggers the Identity Selector using XHTML code or HTML object tags. After the Identity Selector has been triggered, it retrieves the SP's security policy from the SP-STS in step 3 [137].

In step 4 the Identity Selector matches the SP's security policy against the Info-Cards possessed by the user in order to find one that satisfies it. If one or more suitable InfoCards are found, the user is prompted to select one of them. After the user has selected an InfoCard, the Identity Selector initiates a connection with the IdP that issued that InfoCard, and retrieves the IdP security policy in step 5. In step 6, the user performs an authentication process with the IdP via the Identity Selector. As stated above, the current version of the Identity Selector supports four authentication methods, namely: username/password, Kerberos V5 ticket, X.509 certificate (either software-based or using a smart card), and self-issued SAML 1.1 assertion (generated by the SIP).

Then, in step 7, the Identity Selector requests the IdP to provide a security token that asserts the truth of the claims whose types are listed in the selected InfoCard; this request is sent in a *request security token* (RST) message. The IdP then checks whether its security policy permits it to generate the requested security token. If so, the IdP replies by sending a security token within a *request security token response* (RSTR) message. Finally, the Identity Selector forwards the security token to the SP-STS in step 8 (after, optionally, showing its contents to the user) and, if the SP verifies it successfully, the service is granted in step 9.

As in any ICIM system (see Section 3.3.4.2), the SP will get an assertion from the IdP that the security token was issued to a particular PPID. The SP can verify whether or not the Identity Selector that forwarded the token is its rightful owner using one of the proof-of-rightful-possession methods described in Section 3.3.4.2, namely symmetric, asymmetric, and bearer. If the 'symmetric' proof-of-rightful-possession method is used, then the Identity Selector must inform the IdP which SP the user is trying to access; in CardSpace this approach is called 'auditing mode'. Alternatively, if the 'asymmetric' proof-of-rightful-possession method is used, then the Identity Selector does not need to inform the IdP which SP the user is trying to access; this is called 'non-auditing mode'.

We observe that there is some ambiguity regarding the default proof-of-rightful-possession method in CardSpace. In 2005, Microsoft published two documents [124, 126] stating that if the SP does not specify the proof-of-rightful-possession method then the IdP will assume that the SP is requesting a 'symmetric' proof-of-rightful-possession method (i.e. the default is auditing mode). However, in 2008, Microsoft published a further document [125] stating that if the SP does not specify the proof-of-rightful-possession method, then the Identity Selector will request an 'asymmetric' proof-of-rightful-possession method (i.e. the default is non-auditing mode). In order for the Identity Selector to follow the latter approach, Windows operating system users must install the 'Microsoft .NET Framework 3.1 - Service Pack 1' optional update[6].

The CardSpace identity metasystem relies on a number of Web Services protocols and SOAP. Most of these protocols require the SP to have an STS server (see Section 3.3.4.2) in order to process the messages [21, 108, 135].

The CardSpace message flows are as follows:

---

[6]http://www.microsoft.com/downloads/details.aspx?FamilyID=AB99342F-5D1A-413D-8319-81DA479AB0D7

1. **CEUA → SP** : User clicks on the CardSpace logo on the SP log-in web page

2. **SP → CEUA** : InfoCard Tags (XHTML or HTML object tags), to trigger the Identity Selector

3. **Identity Selector ↔ SP-STS** : Identity Selector retrieves the SP security policy using *WS-MetadataExchange*

4. **Identity Selector ↔ User** : User picks an InfoCard

5. **Identity Selector ↔ IdP-STS** : Identity Selector retrieves the IdP security policy

6. **Identity Selector ↔ IdP** : User Authentication

7. **Identity Selector ↔ IdP-STS** : Identity Selector retrieves security token using *WS-MetadataExchange*

8. **Identity Selector → SP-STS** : Identity Selector forwards the security token (after, optionally, showing its contents to the user)

9. **SP → CEUA** : Welcome, you are now logged in!

The messages in steps 3, 5, 7 and 8 are carried over SOAP (see Section 2.4.3), and must be transmitted over an SSL/TLS channel to preserve their confidentiality. If the SP does employ an STS server, then the messages in steps 3 and 8 will be carried using HTTP over an SSL/TLS channel, since in this case the SP would not be capable of processing the WS-* envelopes that require an STS server to be processed. Moreover, such SPs accept only pure tokens (i.e. not encapsulated within XML envelopes) [125]. The integrity of the security token is guaranteed using an XML-Signature, as part of the WS-Security protocol (see Section 2.4.3).

As in any ICIM system, and as described in Section 3.3.4.2, IdP discovery is performed on the user machine. By selecting an InfoCard, the user locates the IdP to be asked to issue the token, since each InfoCard contains an IdP URI from where the security token can be obtained. As previously discussed, since discovery is performed on the user machine, a malicious SP cannot direct a user to a fake IdP, e.g. to steal the user's authentication credentials.

As discussed in Chapter 3, in an ICIM system the IdP (or the SIP) and the SP use the PPID as a 'secret' user pseudonym. These pseudonyms can be used for authentication purposes. Moreover, identifiers (e.g. PPIDs) are treated as claims, and the SP list of claims to be asserted by the IdP can include identifiers (see Section 3.3.4.2 for further details regarding PPIDs). Hence, since asserting an identifier uniquely identifies a user, and asserting user attributes can support service authorisation, then CardSpace can be used for both authentication and authorisation (see Section 3.3.4.2).

4.2.2   Limitations of CardSpace

CardSpace suffers from a number of limitations; some are shared by all web-based identity management systems (as discussed in section 4.7), and some are specific to CardSpace. In this section we will discuss the CardSpace-specific limitations.

An obvious limitation of CardSpace is that, as mentioned earlier, the Identity Selector only supports four user authentication mechanisms, namely: username/password, Kerberos V5 ticket, X.509 certificate (either software-based or from smart cards), or self-issued SAML 1.1 assertion (generated by the SIP).

A further limitation of CardSpace is that the user is required to present her security credentials to the Identity Selector (e.g. a username/password) for transfer to the IdP every time. That is, even if the user chooses to use the same InfoCard/IdP to access multiple SPs, user authentication must be performed before a token is issued. This means that, as for any ICIM system (as discussed in Section 3.3.4.2), CardSpace does not support SSO. This feature also poses an obstacle to the development of delegation services.

Another limitation is that the CardSpace user-enabling components (such as the Identity Selector) only work with the Microsoft Windows operating systems. However, there are a number of other, very similar, ICIM systems that work on a variety of operating systems, such as Higgins[7](which works on Windows, Mac OS X, Linux, and Google Android), and DigitalMe[8](which works on Mac OS X).

Finally, one of the biggest limitations of CardSpace is that the user can only select one InfoCard to present to an SP within a single working session [47]. This is a potentially difficulty since the user attributes for which the SP requests an assertion might not be covered by any one InfoCard. For example, if a user wants to pay his/her car road tax via an SP web site, the SP might ask for a number of attributes such as credit card information, the car insurance policy number, and the driving licence number. Since each of these attributes is issued by a different authoritative source (see Section 3.2), it is quite possible that no single IdP can provide an assertion for them all. It would thus be both more practical and more logical, if the user could present more than one InfoCard to the SP. An 'attribute-aggregation' solution such as that proposed by Chadwick [48] could address this issue, whilst also helping to preserve user privacy.

4.3 Higgins Project

Higgins is an open source ICIM system. The goals of its designers are to develop cross-platform Identity Selectors and to facilitate interoperability amongst web-based identity management systems. Higgins can integrate identity data from

---

[7]http://www.eclipse.org/higgins
[8]http://code.bandit-project.org/trac/wiki/DigitalMe/Installation/MacSafari

multiple, heterogeneous sources (e.g. LDAP directories, SQL data bases, social net-working web sites, etc.) via a common Context Data Model (CDM). In the Higgins CDM, data sources are called 'contexts', and can be accessed using an Identity Attribute Service (IdAS) managed by IdPs [52]. Another distinguishing feature of Higgins is that it can obtain security tokens from IdPs adhering to SAML SSO profiles.

The Higgins project started in the summer of 2003. In early 2005, Higgins was accepted into the Eclipse Foundation and, in 2006, IBM and Novell announced their participation in the project. Higgins has received contributions from Parity Communications Inc., IBM, Novell, Oracle, Computer Associates, Serena, and Google. Version 1.0 of Higgins was released in 2008, and the most recent version (Higgins 1.1) was partially released in 2009 (Higgins developers plan to release the complete version in 2010).

4.3.1   The Higgins Framework

The Higgins framework is quite similar to the CardSpace framework, discussed in Section 4.2.1. The main difference is that Higgins provides an infrastructure to integrate identity data from multiple sources; by contrast, how identity data is obtained by the IdP is outside the scope of CardSpace, and the implementation details are left to the IdPs. Moreover, in Higgins it is assumed that the authentication service can be separated from the attribute service, which means that an IdP-STS can delegate the storage of user attributes to a separate Attribute Service.

As part of the attribute service separation, Higgins supports a third type of InfoCard called a 'relationship InfoCard' (or r-Card) [174], in addition to the two CardSpace InfoCard types (i.e. self-issued and managed InfoCards). A relationship InfoCard can be either self-issued or managed, and its main distinguishing feature is that it supports a special claim type called 'resource-UDR' (where UDR stands for Uniform Data Reference). A 'self-issued' relationship InfoCard contains both a resource-UDR claim reference and its value. However, in the case of a 'managed' relationship InfoCard, the value of the resource-UDR claim must be retrieved from the issuer IdP.

Unlike most claims, whose value is a literal that can be used directly, the resource-UDR claim value is a 'reference'. The value of the resource-UDR claim must include a Universal Data Identifier (UDI) [157]. A UDI contains the following two data fields:

1. **ContextId**: a URI reference identifying a data source (i.e. a network address for a context).

2. **EntityId**: a URI reference identifying a local object within the context (i.e. a network address for user identity data).

If an SP requests an assertion for the resource-UDR claim, then only relationship InfoCards can be selected by the user. The value of the resource-UDR claim can be used by the SP to discover the context that holds the user attributes, so that it can retrieve them directly. This is potentially useful if the IdP-STS has delegated the storage of the user attributes to a separate Attribute Service. Figure 4.2 shows how a relationship InfoCard can help SPs to locate a context that holds user attributes. As shown in the figure, a relationship InfoCard points to an IdP STS which can generate a token that points to an AS within a context.

Higgins 1.0 offers two types of Identity Selectors (known as Higgins Selectors):

1. **A web browser-embedded Selector**. This is a web-browser JavaScript plug-in that is capable of interacting with a 'stand-alone' Identity Selector

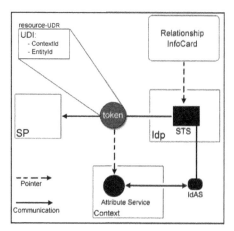

Figure 4.2: Relationship InfoCard

installed on the user machine (e.g. the CardSpace Identity Selector, the Cocoa Higgins Selector (mentioned below), or the DigitalMe Identity Selector) to make use of its user interface. Only Firefox web browsers are supported by this selector (although Microsoft Internet Explorer web browsers are supported by Higgins 1.1).

2. **A stand-alone Selector**. This GTK C++ software is called the 'Cocoa Selector'[9]. It works on the Windows, Linux, and Mac OS X operating systems. Figure 4.3 shows the interface of the Cocoa Higgins Selector on the Mac OS X operating system.

Higgins 1.1 offers an additional stand-alone Identity Selector called the 'AIR-Based Selector'[10]. This Selector has an interface built on Adobe AIR[11], and, as previously stated, it works on the Windows, Mac OS X and Linux operating systems. Higgins developers hope that this selector will replace the current web browser-embedded Selectors that have a number of associated security concerns. Figure 4.4 shows the

[9]http://wiki.eclipse.org/GTK_and_Cocoa_Selector_1.0

Figure 4.3: The interface of the Cocoa Higgins Selector on Mac OS X

interface of the AIR-Based Higgins Selector on Windows.

Higgins 1.1 also offers an Identity Selector for iPhone mobiles[12]. This selector works only with the iPhone operating system[13]. Figure 4.5 shows the interface of the iPhone Higgins Selector.

Finally, Higgins 1.1 introduced the concept of the Higgins Selector Switch (HSS), which provides an abstraction layer that decouples web browser-embedded Higgins Selectors from installed stand-alone Identity Selectors. As shown in figure 4.6, the Higgins web browser-embedded Higgins Selector does not support a specific stand-alone Identity Selector; instead it interacts with the HSS, which is the component responsible for interactions with stand-alone Identity Selectors. The HSS is intended to make the task of developing and improving browser-embedded Higgins Selectors simpler and more consistent across identity selectors.

---

[10]http://wiki.eclipse.org/Adobe_AIR_Selector
[11]http://www.adobe.com/products/air
[12]http://www.apple.com/iphone
[13]http://wiki.eclipse.org/IPhone_Selector

Figure 4.4: The interface of the AIR-Based Higgins Selector on Windows

4.3.2 Limitations of Higgins

As in CardSpace (and all other ICIM systems), SSO is not supported. Moreover, a user can only select one InfoCard to present to an SP within a single working session.

A further limitation is that the Higgins web browser-embedded Selectors rely on the use of JavaScript web browser plug-ins, which have many associated security concerns even if they are digitally signed [2].

4.4 Liberty Alliance Project

The Liberty Alliance project[14] (henceforth abbreviated to Liberty) is an industry collaboration first made public in 2001, at which time it involved 16 major companies including Sun, GM, United Airlines, and France Télécom. Liberty now involves more than 150 members, including government agencies, companies, banks and uni-

---

[14]http://www.projectliberty.org

101

Figure 4.5: The interface of the iPhone Higgins Selector.

versities. In June 2009, the Liberty Alliance announced that its future activities will be taken forward under the umbrella of the Kantara Initiative[15]. According to the project web site on 1st January 2010, there are more than one billion Liberty enabled identities and devices across the world[16].

Liberty aims to build open standard-based specifications for Federated identity management, provide interoperability testing, and to help provide solutions to identity theft. Liberty also aims to establish best practices and business guidelines for federated identity management systems. The Liberty specifications have been adopted by many identity management product vendors, including Sun[17] and Ping Identity[18].

Figure 4.7 shows the general Liberty model. In the example shown in the figure there are two distinct CoTs (see Section 3.3.4.3), and the principal (i.e. the user) has two IdP-issued identities, one for CoT A and one for CoT B, both federated with

---

[15]http://kantarainitiative.org
[16]http://www.projectliberty.org/liberty/resource_center/faq/adoption_1

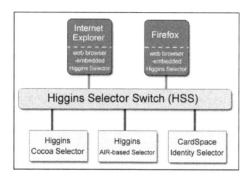

Figure 4.6: Higgins Selector Switch

local identities within the same CoT. These two IdP-issued identities could also be federated, but this would require a pre-established trust relationship between the IdPs.

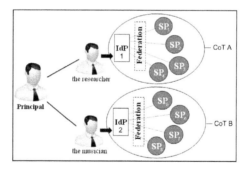

Figure 4.7: The Liberty model

4.4.1 The Liberty Framework

Liberty mandates 'identity federation', and supports the CDC technique for this purpose (see Section 3.3.4.3). The CDC name must contain the string '_liberty_idp', and a base-64 encoded list of the identifiers of all of the IdPs that have issued iden-

---

[17]http://www.sun.com/software/products/identity/standards/liberty.xml
[18]http://www.pingidentity.com

tities to the holding user. Liberty uses long-term pseudonyms, which are typically established between the IdP and the SP during the federation agreement process (see Section 3.3.4.3).

The Liberty specifications are divided into a number of frameworks. Currently, the most mature frameworks are the Identity Federation Framework (ID-FF) [177], and the Identity Web Services Framework (ID-WSF) [173]. In Liberty, as in many federated identity management systems, the authentication and authorisation frameworks are separate.

The ID-FF covers federation and authentication (and supports an SSO service). The main focus of the ID-WSF is the support of identity-based web services (e.g. Geolocation, Contact Book, blogs, calendars, photo sharing, etc.). Originally, the ID-WSF relied on the ID-FF to provide authentication services (and SSO) [80]; however, according to the latest specifications of the ID-WSF authentication SSO services, authentication services (and SSO) can be provided independently using the SAML 2.0 SSO profiles [79]. Almost all the ID-WSF services are built on a user-attribute exchange scheme, which can be regarded as an authorisation framework. We provide here an overview of both the authentication and the authorisation frameworks.

Other Liberty frameworks include the following:

- **The Identity Service Interface Specifications (ID-SIS)** [113]. This provides detailed descriptions of the web services that can be supported by the ID-WSF.

- **Liberty Identity Assurance Framework (LIAF)** [55]. This provides technical details on how to support the OMB/NIST LoA discussed in section 3.3.3.

- **The Identity Governance Framework (IGF)** [119]. This defines security polices for user attribute sharing using the Client Attribute Requirements

Markup Language (CARML) [83], and the Attribute Authority Policy Markup Language (AAPML) [128].

4.4.1.1 The Authentication Framework

The ID-FF specifications support identity federation and authentication (with SSO). They also describe the required techniques, including session management and identity/account linkage.

In order to realise this framework, a set of profiles is required (so called ID-FF Liberty profiles). An ID-FF Liberty profile may best be defined as the combination of message content specifications and message transport mechanisms for a single type of client (that is, a user agent) [39].

There are many types of ID-FF Liberty profile, including SSO and Federation Profiles, Register Name Identifier Profiles, Identity Federation Termination Notification Profiles, Single Logout (or Single Sign-out) Profiles, Identity Provider Introduction, NameIdentifier Mapping Profile and NameIdentifier Encryption Profile. In this thesis we are primarily concerned with the SSO and Federation Profiles. The currently defined SSO and Federation profiles are the Artifact profile, the Browser POST profile, and the Liberty-enabled client and proxy (LEC) profile [39].

These profiles are specified in the version 1.2 of the ID-FF specifications [41, 177], and they rely on SAML assertions as the sole supported format for security tokens. The ID-FF is built on the SAML 1.1 SSO profiles with a number of added extensions. These extensions were later adopted by OASIS, and integrated into SAML 2.0. However, ID-FF is not completely compatible with the SAML 2.0 SSO profiles; there are a small number of technical differences. These differences have been listed on the SAML web site[19]. The ID-FF SSO and Federation profiles adopt the SAML three proof-of-rightful-possession (or subject confirmation) methods, namely HoK, Sender-Vouches, and Bearer (see Section 3.3.4.3).

In Liberty, the authentication process is performed either using the ID-FF SSO profiles, or using the ID-WSF authentication service which is built in the SAML 2.0 SSO profiles.

In this section we describe each of the three ID-FF SSO profiles. These profiles are similar to the SAML 2.0 SSO profiles.

ID-FF Artifact Profile. This framework does not require an enabling software component to be installed on the user machine; it only requires the user to possess a user agent (i.e. a web browser). Figure 4.8 presents a sketch of the message flows within this profile in the case where the user has already been authenticated by the IdP. Note that the IdP can choose any authentication method in accordance with its security policy (see Section 3.3.1). The message flows within the ID-FF Artifact profile are as follows:

1. **User Agent → SP** : Log-in Request

2. **SP** : Obtains IdP (e.g. using CDC)

3. **SP → User Agent → IdP** : Authentication Request (redirect – HTTP GET or POST)

4. **IdP → User Agent → SP** : Authentication Response + SAMLart (redirect – HTTP GET or POST)

5. **SP → IdP** : SAMLart

6. **IdP → SP** : SAML-Assertion Response

7. **SP → User Agent** : Log-in Granted!

106

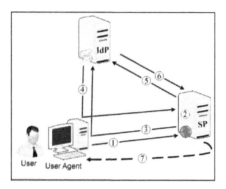

Figure 4.8: The ID-FF Artifact profile message flow

As shown in the message flows above, in the first step the user tries to log-in to the SP. In step 2, the SP obtains the identity of the IdP. How the SP achieves this is not specified. However, the specifications suggest the use of the CDC technique described in Section 3.3.4.3. Alternatively, the SP could use the WAYF technique described in Section 3.3.4.3. In either case IdP discovery is implemented by the SP server.

In steps 3 and 4, the SP and the IdP communicate indirectly by redirecting the user agent (i.e. the web browser) from one party's web site to the other. This redirection is used to carry an Authentication Request message (containing a SAML authentication assertion request), from the SP to the IdP, and an Authentication Response message containing a SAMLart from the IdP to the SP. These messages are embedded within the HTTP GET or POST protocol text.

SAMLart is a SAML artifact that functions as a reference to a specific SAML assertion. This artifact is used later in steps 5 and 6, in which the SP communicates directly with the IdP to obtain the requested SAML assertion. If the SP finds this assertion acceptable, the user will be logged-in in step 7. Messages in steps 4 and 6

---

[19]http://saml.xml.org/differences-between-saml-v2-0-and-liberty-id-ff-1-2

must be digitally signed by the IdP.

Steps 5 and 6 are bound to SOAP, which is carried over an SSL connection to provide confidentiality (integrity is preserved using an XML-Signature). Note that if the user has not been authenticated by the IdP prior to the SP log-in attempt, then the IdP must authenticate the user prior to step 3.

ID-FF Browser POST Profile. The ID-FF Browser POST profile, like the artifact profile, does not require an enabling software component to be installed on the user machine.

Figure 4.9 presents a sketch of the message flows within the ID-FF Browser POST profile in the case where the user has already been authenticated by the IdP. Note that the IdP can choose any authentication method according to its security policy (see Section 3.3.1). The message flows within the ID-FF Browser POST profile are as follows.

1. **User Agent → SP** : Log-in Request

2. **SP** : Obtains IdP (e.g. using CDC)

3. **SP → User Agent → IdP** : Authentication Request (redirect – HTTP GET or POST)

4. **IdP → User Agent → SP** : Authentication Response + SAML-Assertion (within HTML Form, Redirect – HTTP POST)

5. **SP → User Agent** : Log-in Granted!

The message flows within this profile are similar to those within the ID-FF Artifact profile. The main difference is that, in this profile, the SAML messages (i.e. the SAML assertion request and response) are embedded within a hidden HTML

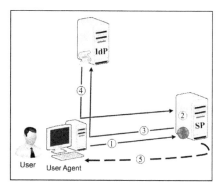

Figure 4.9: The ID-FF Bowser POST profile message flow

form, so there is no need to use an artifact. Hence, there is no need for direct communication between the SP and IdP.

How the SP obtains the identity of the IdP in step 2 is up to the SP. However, the specifications suggest use of the CDC technique described in Section 3.3.4.3. Alternatively, the SP could use the WAYF technique described in Section 3.3.4.3. Again, in either case IdP discovery is implemented by the SP server.

ID-FF LEC Profile. This profile requires the involvement of a Liberty-Enabled User Agent (LEUA) in order to act upon the messages sent and received during the federation and authentication processes. An LEUA is typically implemented as a web browser enhanced with JavaScript components installed on the user machine; such components can be downloaded freely from the Internet (e.g. the SecureID ID-FF 1.1 and ID-FF 1.2 Java Toolkits[20], and the Sun FederationSPAdapter[21]).

Figure 4.10 presents a sketch of the message flows within the ID-FF LEC profile in the case where the user has already been authenticated by the IdP. Note that the IdP

---

[20]http://www.sourceid.org
[21]http://docs.sun.com/source/819-4682

can choose any authentication method according to its security policy (see Section 3.3.1). The Liberty-Enabling component must be installed on the user machine prior to the steps shown in the figure.

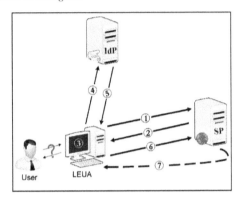

Figure 4.10: The ID-FF LEC profile message flow

The message flows within the ID-FF LEC profile are as follows.

1. **LEUA → SP** : Log-in Request (HTTP Request with Liberty Enabled Header)

2. **SP → LEUA** : Authentication Request + 'optionally' an IdP List

3. **LEUA or User** : Obtains IdP

4. **LEUA → IdP** : Authentication Request

5. **IdP → LEUA** : Authentication Response + SAML-Assertion

6. **LEUA → SP** : Authentication Response + SAML-Assertion

7. **SP → LEUA** : Log-in Granted!

In step 1, the Liberty-enabling components add a special *Liberty Enabled* header to the HTTP request, so that the SP knows that the requesting user agent is Liberty-enabled. In step 2, the SP replies with a special Authentication Request message, which may include a list of trusted IdPs in addition to the SAML authentication assertion request. A brief example of this message is given in Figure 4.11.

```
<lib:AuthnRequestEnvelope
xmlns:lib="urn:liberty:iff:2003-08">

  <lib:AuthnRequest >
   . . . the authentication request
   + a SAML authentication assertion request . . .
  </lib:AuthnRequest>

  <lib:AssertionConsumerServiceURL>
    https://SP.com/LibertyLogin
  </lib:AssertionConsumerServiceURL>

  <lib:IDPList >
   . . . Optional IdP list goes here . . .
  </lib:IDPList>

</lib:AuthnRequestEnvelope>
```

Figure 4.11: An Authentication Request message

The Liberty Specifications do not dictate how the user (or the LEUA) determines the identity of the IdP in step 3; this is left to the implementors of the Liberty-enabling components. However it is implemented, IdP discovery must be implemented on the user machine.

In step 4, the LEUA forwards the Authentication Request message to the IdP. Since the user has already been authenticated by the IdP, the IdP now sends a digitally signed Authentication Response message to the LEUA in step 5. This message is forwarded to the SP in step 6. Finally, the SP checks the forwarded Authentication Response message and, if it is acceptable, the user will be logged-in in step 7.

Messages in steps 4 and 5 must be carried over an SSL connection to provide confidentiality (integrity is guaranteed using an XML-Signature).

In Figure 4.12 we provide an example of a Liberty Authentication Response message. The message shown in the figure is tagged as <Lib:AuthResponse>, and it has a unique identifier (unique to the IdP). It also contains the unique identifier of the

111

Liberty Authentication Request message (unique to the SP) to which it is a response. The issuer of the message is (http://IdP.com), i.e. the URL of the issuer IdP, and this functions as the identifier of the IdP. Similarly, the SP's URL is (http://SP.com), which functions as the identifier of the SP.

```
<lib:AuthnResponse ResponseID="IhUj980QnjdbCsv43M099Rp"
InResponseTo="nK665GfTRE39nmKsbnv" MajorVersion="1" MinorVersion="2"
consent="urn:liberty:consent:obtained" IssueInstant="2010-01-01T23:50:41Z ">
     <samlp:Status>
          <samlp:StatusCode Value="samlp:Success"/>
     </samlp:Status>
<lib:Assertion MajorVersion="1" MinorVersion="2"
AssertionID="ref9393-fgvbvr-483jffhg0nfffoo9"
Issuer="http://IdP.com" IssueInstant="2010-01-01T11:32:49Z"
InResponseTo="vcbf76-urhhf8878-hgjuttee-1df34ghy">
     <saml:Conditions NotBefore="2010-01-01T11:32:49Z" -
     NotOnOrAfter="2010-01-02T12:00:00Z">
          <saml:AudienceRestrictionCondition >
               <saml:Audience>http://SP.com</sam l:Audience>
          </saml:AudienceRestrictionCondition>
     </saml:Conditions>
       <lib:AuthenticationStatement AuthenticationInstant="2010-01-01T08:15:04Z"
          SessionIndex="3" ReauthenticateOnOrAfter="2010-01-01T10:25:17Z"
          AuthenticationMethod="urn:oasis :names:tc:SAML:1.0:am:pa ssword">
               <lib:Subject>
                    <saml:NameIdentifier NameQualifier="http://SP.com"
                    Format="urn:liberty:iff:nam eid:federated">nbbhvg-uyjy5f9-bfg5658hj
                    </saml: NameIdentifier>
                         <saml:SubjectConfirmation>
                              <saml:ConfirmationMethod>urn:oasis:names:tc:SAM
                              L:1.0:cm:bearer</saml:Conf irmationMethod>
                         </saml:SubjectConfirmation>
                    <IDPProvidedNameIdentifier NameQualifier="http://SP.com"
                    Format="urn:liberty:iff:nam eid:federated">nbbhvg-uyjy5f9-bfg5658hj
                    </IDPPro videdNameIdentifier>
               </lib:Subject>
          </lib:AuthenticationStatement>
     <ds:Signature>...</ds:Signature>
     </lib:Assertion>
<lib:ProviderID>http://IdP.com</lib: ProviderID>
<RelayState>nbhgjHhgpp764GGFHNVcfHgTjjdh9847JnHjKLDDGH184jN</ RelayState>
</lib:AuthnResponse>
```

Figure 4.12: Liberty Authentication Response message

As stated above, this message contains a *Liberty assertion* (or <lib:Assertion>) which itself contains a *Liberty authentication statement* (or <lib:AuthenticationSt atement>) which is an enhanced SAML authentication statement. The Liberty assertion has a unique identifier, and it also contains the unique identifier of the Liberty assertion request message to which it is a response. In addition it specifies the duration of its validity; in the example it is valid between 11:32:49 on the 1st of January 2010, and 12:00:00 on the 2nd of January 2010. Within the Liberty assertion is the `<lib:Subject>` element, which contains a shared pseudonym for the user. The assertion also contains the `<SubjectConfirmation>` element, which specifies the proof-of-rightful-possession method that has been used (in this case the Bearer method). Finally, the IdP's digital signature is included in the `<ds:Signature>` element.

4.4.1.2   The Authorisation Framework

The ID-WSF builds upon the ID-FF to provide a framework for identity-based web services in a federated network identity environment. As stated in 4.4.1, the ID-WSF originally relied on the ID-FF to provide authentication services (and SSO) [80]. However, according to the latest specifications of the ID-WSF authentication SSO services, authentication services (and SSO) can be provided independently using the SAML 2.0 SSO profiles [79].

The People Service is one of the services offered by the ID-WSF [118]. This service provides a method by which a user can create an account with another user's SP to view pre-identified shared files. This gives a limited degree of support for functionality which might normally be supported by a delegation system, but it is not a full delegation service.

The ID-WSF supports user attribute sharing between SPs and/or between an IdP and SPs within the same CoT [173]. Thus the ID-WSF can be regarded as an authorisation framework. In this section we provide a brief overview of the ID-WSF user attribute sharing model.

Before describing the attribute sharing model, we first consider the *Discovery Service* (DS) for the ID-WSF [31]. This service is typically managed by the IdP, and is designed to help SPs find a specific web service provider by providing them with a list of endpoint references (or EPRs), i.e. network resolvable addresses of web service providers. This is distinct from the IdP discovery service discussed in Chapter 3.

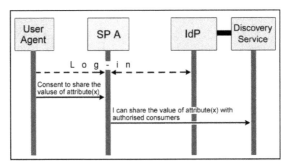

Figure 4.13: User attribute registration with the Discovery Service

In order for an SP (or an IdP) to be able to share a given user attribute, it must first register this attribute with the DS. Figure 4.13 presents an example of the message flows for the user attribute registration process. In this example it is assumed that the user has federated his/her SP-issued identity with his/her IdP-issued identity, and that the user has already been successfully authenticated by the IdP. The user first logs-in to an SP (SP A), using the ID-WSF authentication service built on SAML 2.0 SSO profiles (or one of the ID-FF Federation and SSO profiles described in 4.4.1.1). The network resolvable address of the user's DS is included in the Liberty Authentication Response message, which means that SP A can now locate and communicate with the DS. The user then asks SP A, via the user agent, to share one (or more) attributes registered with SP A (attribute x, say) with other SPs in the same CoT. Finally, SP A sends a message to the DS asking it to associate specific metadata (in this example, the user attribute x) with a specific user. Subsequently, when other SPs in the same CoT query the DS about where to find a service that can provide the value of the user's attribute x to authorised consumers, they will receive EPRs pointing to SP A.

114

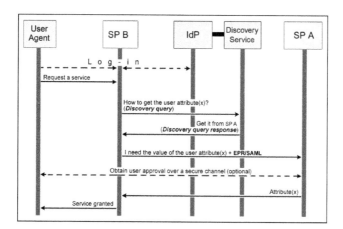

Figure 4.14: User attribute sharing in the ID-WSF

Figure 4.14 presents an example of message flows for user attribute sharing in the ID-WSF. In this example it is assumed that the user has federated his/her SP-issued identities with his/her IdP-issued identity, the user has already been successfully authenticated by the IdP, and that the location of the service which can provide the value of the user's attribute x to authorised consumers has been already registered with the DS. The user first logs-in to an SP (SP B), using the ID-WSF authentication service built on the SAML 2.0 SSO profiles (or one of the ID-FF Federation and SSO profiles described in 4.4.1.1). The network resolvable address of the user's DS is included in the Liberty Authentication Response message, which means that SP B can now locate and communicate with the DS. The user then requests a service from SP B. SP B now discovers that it needs to obtain the value of the user attribute x in order to authorise access to the requested service. To achieve this, SP B sends a *Discovery Query* message to the DS asking whether or not the location of a service that can provide the value of the user's attribute x to authorised consumers has been registered.

Subsequently, the DS sends a *Discovery query response* message to SP B saying that user attribute x can be obtained from SP A, along with an EPR pointing to SP A. This EPR is conveyed within a signed SAML assertion (version 2 or 1.x). Moreover, the DS performs an automatic mapping of the user pseudonyms (i.e. PIDs), and includes an encrypted version of the user's PID (i.e. the pseudonym shared by the IdP and SP A) in the EPR so that SP A can identify the user. Note that the ID-WSF specifications do not dictate the choice of encryption scheme, so this assertion could, for example, be encrypted using a public key of SP A or a secret key shared by the IdP and SP A. After receiving the *Discovery query response* message, SP B forwards the received EPR to SP A. SP A then decrypts the user's PID, and identifies the user using the shared pseudonym. SP A now sends the value of the user attribute x to SP B, which, finally, grants the user access to the requested service.

4.4.2   Limitations of Liberty

One of the most significant limitations of Liberty is that, in the Artifact and Browser POST Profiles, IdP discovery is performed by the SP server. This means that a malicious SP could redirect a user to a fake IdP web site, which could then steal the user's security credentials. However, such an attack is not possible if the LEC profile is used.

Another limitation is that the IdP is made aware of all the SPs the user tries to access. This enables the IdP to track user activities, which could be a threat to user privacy (depending on the application scenario).

Finally, the fact that only one IdP can be queried in single working session (i.e. attribute-aggregation is not supported) is a major limitation of Liberty.

4.5 Shibboleth Project

The Shibboleth project[22] has overseen the development of an open source Federated identity management system. The system has been developed by the Internet2 consortium[23], and offers standards-based authentication and authorisation frameworks (including an SSO service). In August 2008, Shibboleth superseded Athens[24] as the JISC-preferred federated identity management system for use by UK educational establishments[25].

Development of Shibboleth started in 2000, and Shibboleth 1.0 was released in July 2003. Subsequently, Shibboleth 1.3 was released in August 2005, and Shibboleth 2.0 (the current version) in March 2008. Shibboleth 2.0 is backward compatible with Shibboleth 1.3.

Whilst the current version of Shibboleth does not support delegation, a draft specification supporting such functionality has been published. This is described in section 4.8.2.1 below.

4.5.1 The Shibboleth Framework

Shibboleth 1.x uses SAML 1.1 assertions as the syntax for security tokens [44, 131], whereas Shibboleth 2.0 supports both SAML 1.1 and SAML 2.0 assertions[26].

Shibboleth mandates 'identity federation' (see Section 3.3.4.3), in which the IdP and the SP exchange their public key certificates. Unlike in Liberty, the IdP and the SP do not have to establish long-term shared pseudonyms during the federation

---

[22]http://shibboleth.internet2.edu
[23]http://www.internet2.org
[24]http://www.athens.ac.uk
[25]http://www.jisc.ac.uk/whatwedo/programmes/amtransition/iamsp.aspx
[26]http://shibboleth.internet2.edu/shib-v2.0.html

process (but they can if they wish) [35]. Instead of long-term pseudonyms, the IdP
and SP can use short-term random IDs to help preserve user privacy and maintain
anonymity [35].

Although Shibboleth supports the SAML proof-of-rightful-possession methods (i.e.
HoK, Sender-Vouches, and Bearer), implementing these methods is not mandatory
(i.e. the SAML assertion is not required to contain a proof-of-rightful-possession field
if the SP does not mandate it) [44].

Unlike Liberty, the Shibboleth specifications do not include a stand-alone LoA framework. However, since Shibboleth 2.0 is built on SAML 2.0, an IdP can embed LoA
information within a SAML 2.0 assertion[27].

In Shibboleth 1.x, the authentication and authorisation frameworks are separate;
however, in Shibboleth 2.0, they can be combined into single framework. We discuss
these frameworks in greater detail below.

4.5.1.1 The Authentication Framework

The Shibboleth authentication framework is essentially an SSO framework, and is
similar to the Liberty authentication framework discussed earlier in this chapter.
Shibboleth 2.0 supports the Browser POST, Artifact, and ECP SAML SSO profiles,
whereas Shibboleth 1.x only supports the SAML Browser POST profile (see Section
2.4.2).

In Shibboleth, the IdP component responsible for authenticating the user and issuing
authentication assertions for use by SPs, is called the Authentication Service (AS).
The AS is also responsible for generating temporary IDs for users in the form of

---

[27]https://spaces.internet2.edu/display/SHIB/LevelOfAssurance

short-term pseudonyms or opaque handles (if long-term pseudonyms are not used). The Attribute Authority Service (AAS) is an IdP component responsible for user attribute management.

IdP discovery is performed by the SP server. It is typically achieved using the WAYF technique (see Section 3.3.4.3); however, the SP could use any IdP discovery technique [44]. The message flows within the Shibboleth authentication framework are as follows:

1. **User Agent → SP**: Service Request

2. **SP → User Agent → SP-WAYF Service**: GET the SP-WAYF Service web page (redirect – HTTP GET)

3. **User → User Agent → SP-WAYF Service**: User selects an IdP from the WAYF IdP list via the User Agent

4. **SP-WAYF Service → User Agent → IdP-AS**: Authentication Request (redirect – HTTP GET or POST)

5. **User Agent ↔ IdP-AS**: User Authentication

6. **IdP-AS → IdP-AAS + IdP-AS → User Agent → SP**: IdP-AS shares the user temporary ID with the IdP-AAS and the SP, and sends an Authentication Response to the SP along with the IdP-AAS location (within HTML Form, redirect – HTTP POST)

7. **SP → User Agent**: You have been authenticated!

Figure 4.15 gives an outline of the message flows within the Shibboleth authentication framework. In the first step, the user requests a service from the SP (e.g. access to a document) via the user agent; then, in step 2, the SP redirects the user agent to its WAYF service to determine the IdP. In step 3, the user selects an IdP from the list shown on the WAYF service web page (figure 4.16 gives an example of such a WAYF service web page).

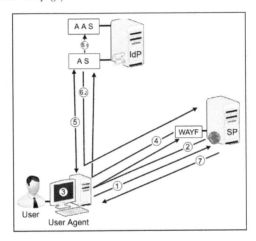

Figure 4.15: The message flows of the Shibboleth authentication framework

Figure 4.16: An example of the user interface of a WAYF service web page

In step 4, the WAYF service redirects the user agent to the IdP-AS, simultaneously passing the IdP-AS an embedded Authentication Request message (which includes a SAML authentication assertion query). On receipt of the redirection, in step 5 the IdP-AS authenticates the user (if the user has not already been authenticated) using an authentication method of its choice. If the authentication is successful, the IdP-AS creates the requested SAML authentication assertion and a short-term

120

random ID for the user. The IdP-AS shares this ID with the ID-AAS, and sends an Authentication Response message (which includes the created assertion) to the SP in step 6, embedded within a hidden HTML form. The message must be signed by the IdP and should contain the address of the IdP-AAS, so that the SP can request user attribute assertions from it when using the authorisation framework. If the IdP and the SP have shared pseudonyms for the user prior to the execution of the framework, then the SP-issued pseudonym is included in the authentication assertion; otherwise, a random ID is included. Finally, after receiving the Authentication Response message, the SP checks its contents and the validity of the signature. If the signature is valid, then the user is deemed to be authenticated by the SP.

4.5.1.2 The Authorisation Framework

As stated above, this framework can be optionally combined with the authentication framework in Shibboleth 2.0. If we assume that the authentication process has already been executed in the current working session, then the message flows of the authorisation framework are as follows:

1. **User Agent → SP**: Service Request

2. **SP → IdP-AAS**: Attribute Assertion Request

3. **Id-AAS → SP**: Attribute Assertion Response

4. **SP → User Agent** : Service Granted!

Figure 4.17 gives an outline of the message flows within the Shibboleth authorisation framework. After the user requests a service (e.g. access to a specific document) via the user agent in step 1, the SP sends an Attribute Request message (which includes a SAML attribute assertion query) to the IdP-AAS in step 2. The SP already knows

the network resolvable address of the IdP-AAS, since it obtained it from the IdP-AS
during the authentication procedure. In addition to a list of the attributes for which
the SP requires an assertion, the Attribute Request message includes the short-term
random user ID that the SP received from the IdP-AS during the authentication
procedure (note that the IdP-AAS also received this ID from the IdP-AS). In step
3, the IdP-AAS checks whether or not the Attribute Release Policies (discussed
below) allow it to share the values of the requested attributes with the SP and, if
so, it sends them to the SP within an Attribute Assertion Response message (which
includes a signed SAML attribute assertion). Finally, the SP checks the validity of
the received Attribute Assertion Response message, and if valid, checks whether or
not the received values allow the user to be granted access to the requested service;
if so, the user is granted the requested service in step 4. The messages sent in steps
2 and 4 must be carried over a secure channel (e.g. as provided by SSL/TLS) to
preserve their confidentiality.

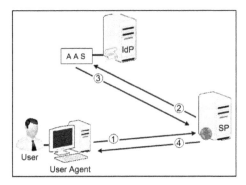

Figure 4.17: The message flows of the Shibboleth authorisation framework

The Shibboleth authorisation framework relies on the use of Attribute Release Policies (ARPs) to control the release of user attributes. ARPs are written in XML, and
are used by the IdP-AAS to express the user attribute release rules (i.e. an ARP
indicates which user attributes can be released to which SP) [36].

Typically, an ARP is created for each user by the IdP-AAS. An ARP contains a list of rules, where each rule consists of the following fields [47].

- **A destination SP identifier**. This identifier is typically the SP's network resolvable address or URL (e.g. https://SP.com).

- **A list of attribute types (and optionally specific attribute values)**. This specifies the attributes that can be released to the SP identified in the previous field.

- **Other optional conditions**. This is used to specify other conditions on release, e.g. the time of day, location of the user, etc.

When the IdP-AAS receives the Attribute Request message from an SP in step 2 of the authorisation framework, it extracts the SP's URL from the SAML attribute assertion query. Using this URL the IdP-AAS searches the relevant ARP to find the rules associated with this SP, and then checks whether or not the request attribute can be released.

Figure 4.18 presents an example of an ARP that includes two rules. The first rule permits the IdP-AAS to release the user attribute, *PersonPrincipalName*, to a specific SP, i.e. *https://SP.com*. The value of this attribute is not specified in the rule, so it can be any value chosen by the IdP-AAS. The second rule permits the IdP-AAS to release the user attribute, *PersonAffiliation*, to any SP. The released attribute value must be as specified in the rule, i.e. *Waleed@isg.rhul.ac.uk*.

As shown in figure 4.18, the `<Target>` element has a single child element, either `<Requester>` or `<AnyTarget/>`. The `<Requester>` element must contain a matching function reference and the identifier of an SP to match against. Two matching function references are defined, namely *regexMatch*, indicating a regular expression, and *exactShar*, indicating that the rule applies only to the SP whose identifier exactly

```
<?xml version="1.0" encoding="UTF-8"?>
<AttributeReleasePolicy xmlns:xsi="http://www.w3.org/2001/XMLSchema-instance"
xmlns="urn:mace:shibboleth:arp:1.0"
xsi:schemaLocation="urn:mace:shibboleth:arp:1.0 shibboleth-arp-1.0.xsd" >

    <Description>... A description of the ARP ...</Description>

    <Rule>
        <Target>
            <Requester
            matchFunction="urn:mace:shibboleth:arp:matchFunction:exactShar">
            https://SP1.com</Requester>
        </Target>
        <Attribute name="urn:mace:dir:attribute-def:eduPersonPrincipalName">
            <AnyValue release="permit"/>
        </Attribute>
    </Rule>

    <Rule>
        <Target>
            <AnyTarget/>
        </Target>
        <Attribute name="urn:mace:dir:attribute-def:eduPersonAffiliation">
            <Value release="permit">Waleed@isg.rhul.ac.uk</Value>
        </Attribute>
    </Rule>

</AttributeReleasePolicy>
```

Figure 4.18: An example ARP

matches that specified. The `<AnyTarget/>` element indicates that the user attribute specified in the rule can be released to any SP.

The `<Attribute>` element specifies the user attribute for which the rule has been created, and whether or not the value of this attribute can be released to the SP specified in the `<Target>` element. Optionally, it can also contain a specific value for the attribute. If the default rule in the IdP-AAS is to deny the release of all user attributes, then the `<Attribute>` element will, if present, contain the word 'Permit' to indicate that the specified attribute can be released to the specified target (or targets). Similarly, if the default rule is to permit the release all of the user attributes, then the `<Attribute>` element will, if present, contain the word 'Deny' to indicate that the specified attribute cannot be released to the specified target (or targets).

There are two types of ARPs, namely *site* ARPs and *user* ARPs. A site ARP pertains to all the users of the IdP-AAS, whereas a user ARP applies only to an individual user. User ARPs can be maintained either by the IdP administrator or by the users themselves, according to the IdP local policy [47]. If two ARPs apply to a particular user at the same time (i.e. the site ARP and a user ARP), then both ARPs must permit the release of a given user attribute to an SP before it can be released.

The Shibboleth Attribute Release Policy Editor (ShARPE)[28] is an open source GUI ARP editor developed by the MAMS project[29]. This editor provides a user-friendly interface enabling both users and IdP administrators to construct ARPs.

ARPs are held in XML files (each file contains only one ARP), and the locations of these files must be specified in *idp.xml*, the Shibboleth IdP main configuration file, which must be located in the 'etc' folder of the Shibboleth IdP server. The `<ArpRepository>` element in the configuration file defines the type of ARP processing, and the path to the ARP directory [36]. The site ARP must be called *arp.site.xml*, and user ARPs must be called *arp.user.$PRINCIPALNAME.xml*, where *$PRINCIPALNAME* is the name of the relevant user.

4.5.2 Limitations of Shibboleth

One of the most significant security limitations of Shibboleth is that IdP discovery is performed on the SP server. This fact, as discussed in 4.4.2, could be exploited by a malicious SP to redirect a user to a fake IdP web site, which could then obtain the user's security credentials.

---

[28]http://www.federation.org.au/twiki/bin/view/Federation/ShARPE
[29]https://mams.melcoe.mq.edu.au/zope/mams

Moreover, the use of proof-of-rightful-possession methods is optional [44]. Thus an IdP might not provide a user with the means to prove rightful possession of a security token to an SP. Such an approach increases the risk of an impostor using a stolen token to gain access to SP resources.

A further limitation of Shibboleth is that, for any given IdP, the authorisation framework only allows a single attribute authority (i.e. the AAS) to be queried for user attributes. It would enhance practicality if SPs were capable of obtaining user attributes from more than one independent attribute authority to be used in association with a particular IdP. In addition, attribute-aggregation is not supported.

Finally, the Shibboleth specifications do not support Single Sign-off (see Section 3.3.2). As a result, in order to terminate every open session, a user must sign-off from the IdP and from every SP to which the user signed on, adversely affecting Shibboleth's usability and security.

4.6 OpenID

OpenID is an open source identity management system in which IdPs issue their users with 'global' identifiers that can be used to log-in to any SP. Although OpenID fits the conceptual model described in Section 3.3.1, OpenID is neither a Federated nor an Information Card-based identity management system (using the terms as defined in Section 3.3.4), since it relies on a different model (described below).

The first version of OpenID was released in 2005, and the most recent version is 2.0 [150] (released in December 2007). OpenID is owned and managed by the OpenID Foundation[30], and is supported by many well-known organisations including Google,

---

[30]http://openid.net/foundation

IBM, Microsoft, Yahoo!, PayPal, and VeriSign. According to the OpenID web site, there are currently over one billion OpenID-enabled identities, and approximately nine million OpenID-enabled SPs on the Internet[31]. However, almost none of these SPs provide access to any information of any real value (although this may change in the future). In the remainder of this section we describe the OpenID framework in greater detail.

4.6.1   The OpenID Framework

In the OpenID framework, an IdP issues a user with a global identifier (or OpenID) that can be used to log-in to any OpenID-enabled SP. This identifier is usually a URI (e.g. a URL), and is used to discover the IdP that issued it. Obviously, there is no need for pseudonyms in this framework, since IdPs and the SPs can refer to a user using the OpenID global identifier.

There is no identity federation process in OpenID; however, if a user already holds an SP-issued identifier, then the SP may choose to 'locally' link this identifier with the user OpenID (i.e. the IdP-issued global identifier).

The OpenID specifications include an LoA framework that supports the OMB/NIST assurance levels (see Section 3.3.3) [28]. This LoA framework enables IdPs and SPs to define their own 'custom' assurance levels.

The OpenID authentication and authorisation frameworks are separate. We discuss these frameworks in greater detail below.

Finally, we observe that OpenID does not support any proof-of-rightful-possession methods [78].

---

[31]http://openid.net/2009/12/16/openid-2009-year-in-review

4.6.1.1   The Authentication Framework

The OpenID authentication framework is essentially an SSO framework; however, it is not built on SAML assertions or on the SAML SSO profiles [150]. Figure 4.19 sketches the message flows within the OpenID authentication framework. The message flows within this framework are as follows:

1. **User Agent → SP**: Log-in Request (the user must enter her OpenID)

2. **SP**: Obtains IdP

3. **SP ↔ IdP**: Optionally, the SP establishes a secret with the IdP using DHKE

4. **SP → User Agent → IdP**: Authentication Request (redirect – HTTP GET)

5. **User Agent ↔ IdP**: User Authentication

6. **IdP → User Agent → SP**: Authentication Response (within HTML Form, redirect – HTTP POST)

7. **SP ↔ IdP**: Optionally, the SP checks the validity status of the token with the IdP

8. **SP → User Agent**: Log-in Granted!

In the first step, the user tries to log-in to the SP web site via the user agent. The user must enter her OpenID as her identifier in the log-in form. The OpenID can be either a URL or an Extensible Resource Identifier (XRI) [151], an abstract and domain-independent identifier. The URI and the Internationalized Resource Identifier (IRI) [60] standards are compatible with XRI.

The SP then obtains the identity of the IdP in step 2. The IdP discovery technique depends on the type of the user OpenID, as described below.

- If the OpenID is an **XRI**, then the SP performs the 'XRI Resolution' protocol [175] via HTTP(S) URIs. The protocol execution should output an eXtensible

Resource Descriptor Sequence (XRDS) [74] document that contains the IdP network resolvable address.

- If the OpenID is a **URL**, then:

  – the SP performs the Yadis protocol [127], which uses the OpenID (i.e. the URL) to HTTP GET an XRDS document containing the IdP network resolvable address from a remote server. If the Yadis protocol does not find an XRDS document, then

  – the SP performs an HTML-based discovery, in which the SP fetches an HTML document stored at the same URL. The <HEAD> element of this HTML document must contain a <LINK> element with two attributes, *rel* set to 'openid2.provider', and *href* set to the IdP's URL.

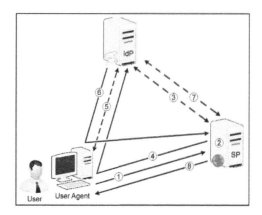

Figure 4.19: The message flows of the OpenID authentication framework

In step 3, the SP optionally establishes a shared secret key with the IdP using the DHKE protocol (see Section 2.4.4). This process is called 'handle association' in the OpenID specifications. In step 4, the SP redirects the user agent to the IdP with an embedded Authentication Request message. If the user has not already been authenticated by the IdP during the current working session, then the IdP authenticates the user in step 5, using an authentication method of its choice.

129

After authenticating the user, the IdP extracts and processes the Authentication Request message. It then redirects the user agent to the SP with an Authentication Response message that contains a MACed authentication token (see Section 2.3.1.2), in step 6. If the SP has performed the 'optional' step 3, or has established a shared secret key with the IdP prior to the protocol run, then this MAC is computed using this secret key, so that the SP can verify the received token and skip step 7. Otherwise, i.e. if the SP has not performed the 'optional' step 3 and has not established a shared secret key with the IdP prior to the protocol run, then the SP must perform step 7, in which it directly sends the token back to the IdP, asking whether or not it is valid. SPs that choose to share a secret key with an IdP are called 'stateful' SPs, whereas SPs that choose not to are called 'stateless' SPs. If the token is valid, then in step 8 the SP permits the user to log-in.

4.6.1.2   The Authorisation Framework

OpenID supports an attribute exchange framework [76], which functions as an authorisation framework. This framework can be used by the SP to retrieve specific user attributes (e.g. an email address) from the IdP, after obtaining the consent of the user to release the requested attributes. Retrieved attributes can be used by the SP to create a local account for the user (i.e. user registration), or to identify a registered user.

Two operations are defined: fetch and store. *Fetch* retrieves user attributes from an IdP, while *store* saves or updates user attributes at an IdP. These operations must be initiated by the SP, and they are passed to the IdP via the user agent as in the OpenID authentication framework. A demonstration of this framework can be found at the Sxip web site[32].

---

[32]https://verify.sxip.com/demorp

4.6.2   Limitations of OpenID

OpenID suffers from a number of security limitations. Of particular concern is its reliance on the notion of global identifiers, which raises significant privacy concerns. According to the W3C P3P (see Section 2.2.7), 'unique identifiers' should be treated as private information. However, in OpenID, user unique identifiers (i.e. OpenIDs) are global by definition, and releasing them to SPs is an essential part of the system. Malicious SPs could collude using the OpenID to trace user activities on the Internet, including the exchange of user preferences, interests and surfing behaviour, e.g. for targeted advertising.

Another limitation is that the IdP discovery is performed on the SP server. As discussed in Sections 4.4.2 and 4.5.2, this could be exploited by a malicious SP to redirect users to a web site masquerading as the IdP, e.g. to obtain their credentials.

A further limitation of OpenID is the lack of attribute-aggregation support (i.e. only one IdP can be queried in single working session).

Finally, as previously mentioned, OpenID does not support any proof-of-rightful-possession methods, increasing the risk of an imposter using a stolen security token to log-in to an SP.

4.7   Shared Security Limitations

In this section, we investigate certain security limitations that are shared by all the identity management systems discussed in this chapter.

4.7.1 Reliance on DNS Names

The first security limitation we observe is a reliance on DNS names (i.e. URLs) as both identifiers and network addresses for IdPs and SPs. If an attacker is able to corrupt a DNS server, it could direct the user agent to a fake web site, which might then be able to obtain the user's security credentials. This problem is very difficult to address. Probably the only long term solution to this problem is to hope that the use of DNSSEC [14], or some other secure address resolution solution, will become widespread.

4.7.2 Judgements of SP Authenticity

The user judgement regarding the authenticity of the SP is a security-critical task in all the identity management systems we have described.

- In a system in which IdP discovery is performed on the SP server (such as Federated identity management systems and OpenID), a malicious SP could redirect users to a web site masquerading as the IdP in order to steal their security credentials. Moreover, the SP will learn that there is a federation relationship between the user and the IdP (in a Federated identity management system), or will obtain the user's OpenID (in OpenID), which functions as a unique global identifier for the user. Unique identifiers can be regarded as private data, and hence this is an undesirable property (see Section 2.2.7.1).

- In an ICIM system, the SP obtains personal information belonging to the user in the form of claims asserted in a security token. Thus, if accepted by a user, a malicious SP could gather sensitive personal information about users. Thus any misjudgement of the authenticity of an SP could result in a serious privacy violation.

In all web-based identity management systems, users are responsible for judging the authenticity of the SP. This typically involves either checking the validity of the SP's SSL/TLS certificate (if the SP has one), or just hoping that the visited SP is as intended, perhaps including a check that the expected URL appears in the address bar of the web browser.

CardSpace and Higgins possess the following user-friendly mechanism which helps to provide guidance to the user regarding the authenticity of the SP. When the user is prompted to provide consent to use a particular InfoCard with an SP for the first time, the user is shown a warning screen which helps in making a judgement regarding the authenticity of this SP. This judgement is based on one of:

1. a high-assurance public key certificate belonging to the SP,

2. an 'ordinary' public key certificate belonging to the SP (e.g. a certificate used for SSL/TLS), or

3. no certificate at all.

Obviously, in the third situation the user has no evidence of the honesty of the SP [34]. Microsoft recommends the first option, i.e. the use of a high assurance certificate [20, 30, 126] (also referred to as a 'higher-value', 'higher-assurance' or 'extended validation' certificate). This is an X.509 certificate that is only issued after a rigorous and well-defined registration process, unlike the CA-specific procedures used for issuing certificates commonly employed as the basis for SSL/TLS security [138]. A high assurance certificate might include a digitally signed bitmap of the SP's company logo, in order to make it easier for the user to identify the certificate holder[33]. Figure 4.20 shows an example of a CardSpace message to the user describing a high assurance certificate issued by 'VeriSign' to a company called 'Overdue Media'. The 'check mark' beside a certificate's field is an indication that the certificate issuer has assurance of the veracity of that field.

In general, it would appear that a typical user is not qualified to make such a security critical decision. Many users do not pay much attention when they are asked to approve a digital certificate, either because they do not understand the importance of the approval decision, or because they know that they must approve the certificate in order to get access to a particular web site. SPs without any certificates at all can be used in web-based identity management systems (given user consent), and this leads to a serious risk of a privacy violation. If we consider the potentially large number of SPs, it is likely that (at least initially) many of them will not possess a high assurance certificate. Even in the case where an SP does have a high assurance certificate and the user is careful, the user may be deceived by a company name or logo that is similar to that used by a legitimate SP (although in principle this should be prevented by the registration process for a high assurance certificate).

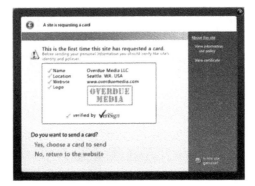

Figure 4.20: An example of a higher-value certificate [34]

Finally, we observe that, as discussed above, the Identity Selector in an ICIM system warns the user when accessing an SP for the first time. Although this warning might

---

[33]The inclusion of a logo is discussed in a number of documents circulated by Microsoft [34, 126], although the latest version of the draft standard for extended validation certificates [30], as published by the CA/Browser Forum, does not mandate the inclusion of a logo. Whether or not such a requirement will be included in the standard at a later date remains unclear.

help the user to detect a false SP, it is not a complete solution. One reason for this is that the identities of visited SPs are stored locally on the user machine. Thus every time a user accesses an SP for the first time via a particular machine a warning will be provided. Thus if a user employs more than one PC[34](e.g. a personal laptop and an office desktop), then repeated warnings will be received for the same SP. Such repetition may result in the user becoming desensitised to the warnings. Also, once an SP has successfully deceived a user, then no warning will be provided on subsequent accesses to the same fraudulent SP.

4.7.3   Reliance on a Single Layer of Authentication

All the identity management systems we have considered rely on authentication of the user by the IdP. In the case where a single IdP and multiple SPs are involved in a single working session, which seems likely to be a typical scenario, the security of the system within that working session will rely on a single layer of authentication, i.e. the authentication of the user to the IdP.

This user authentication can be achieved in a variety of ways (e.g. username/password, X.509 certificate, Kerberos v5 ticket, self-issued token, one-time password, etc.); however, it seems likely that in many cases a simple username/password authentication technique will be used. If a working session is hijacked (e.g. by compromising a Kerberos token), or the password is cracked (e.g. via guessing, brute-force, key logging, or dictionary attacks), then the security of the entire system will be compromised.

One approach to mitigating this vulnerability involves combining two different authentication frameworks during the same working session. For example, before a

---

[34]Indeed, the user should be careful when downloading InfoCards onto multiple PCs. Downloading InfoCards on shared PCs (e.g. in an Internet Café) is clearly unwise.

user agent is able to use an ICIM system, it could be required to be authenticated by OpenID, or vice versa (a similar solution has been proposed in [116], and by others, including Cameron[35]). However, such a solution would clearly make the authentication process more complex, not least for the user, who would be required to maintain credentials for multiple identity management systems. It would also mean that the system would only work in circumstances where both the required identity management systems are available.

4.8 Practicality of Identity Management Systems

One of the main goals of this thesis is to propose novel schemes to enhance the practicality of identity management systems. A variety of approaches can be pursued to enhance practicality; we focus here on two particular directions. The first involves developing integration schemes to enable interoperation between identity management systems. The second is to develop means of delegation, so that a user can delegate to a third party all or subset of its access rights at an SP.

In this section we review prior work on integration and delegation for identity management systems.

4.8.1 Integration

As mentioned in Section 1.1, the lack of interoperability between identity management systems is an obstacle to their practical use; this is especially the case since almost all web-based identity management solutions require several independent entities to participate in the identification and/or authentication process. If the user's

---

[35]http://www.identityblog.com/?p=659

4.8 Practicality of Identity Management Systems

IdP uses one identity management system, and an SP that the user wishes to access uses another incompatible system, then a problem arises. Given the relatively large number of identity management systems that have developed in the last few years, such a scenario is likely to arise frequently; thus system interoperability is a key practical concern.

Both the Bandit and Concordia projects are developing open source integration technologies for web-based identity management systems. As stated in Section 3.3.4.2, the Bandit project has developed DigitalMe, an ICIM system. Bandit also aims to develop integration techniques supporting interoperation between ICIM systems. Bandit and Higgins (see also Section 4.3.1) have ensured that the DigitalMe Identity Selector is seamlessly interoperable with the Higgins Identity Selector.

Project Concordia is a global initiative intended to promote interoperability between web-based identity management systems; recently it joined the Kantara Initiative[36]. Concordia has proposed an interoperation framework for Federated and Information Card-based identity management systems[37]. The scheme covers two types of Federated identity management systems, namely systems built on SAML SSO profiles (or SAML-enabled systems), and systems built on WS-Federation (or WS-Federation-enabled systems). The framework enables users to access SAML-enabled (or WS-Federation-enabled) SPs, even if their IdP is ICIM-enabled. In the case of a SAML-enabled SP, the main parties involved are as follows:

1. A user.

2. An ICIM-enabled user agent.

3. A SAML-enabled SP (e.g. a Liberty-enabled SP); such a party is referred to below as a SAML-SP.

---

[36]http://kantarainitiative.org/confluence/display/concordia/Home
[37]http://projectconcordia.org/index.php/Infocard_Authentication_Scenario_Details

4. A SAML-enabled IdP (e.g. a Liberty-enabled IdP) that must simultaneously act as an ICIM-SP (e.g. a CardSpace-enabled SP); such a party is referred to below as a SAML-IdP/ICIM-SP.

5. An ICIM-enabled IdP (e.g. a CardSpace-enabled IdP); such a party is referred to below as a ICIM-IdP.

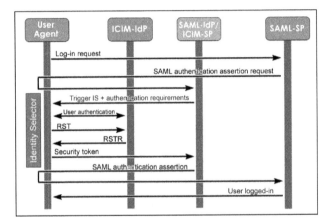

Figure 4.21: ICIM and SAML-enabled systems integration framework

Figure 4.21 provides a sketch of the framework message flows. User authentication involves the following steps:

1. The user tries to log-in to a SAML-SP via a user agent.

2. The SAML-SP redirects the user agent to a SAML-IdP with a SAML authentication assertion request message. This message contains the authentication method that the SAML-SP wants the IdP to use, which must be one of the methods supported by the ICIM system in use.

3. The SAML-IdP/ICIM-SP authenticates the user via an ICIM system and WS-Trust, as required by the SAML-SP. The SAML-IdP converts the attribute requirements specified by the SAML-SP into the corresponding claim type(s)

in order to enable the selection of an appropriate card. If the specified authentication mechanism requires a managed card to be used, then an appropriate managed Infocard must be selected.

4. If a managed Infocard is used, then the Identity Selector sends an RST to the ICIM-IdP, which authenticates the user and responds to the Identity Sector with an RSTR.

5. The Identity Selector sends the RSTR to the SAML-IdP/ICIM-SP.

6. The SAML-IdP/ICIM-SP redirects the user agent back to the SAML-SP, specifying the authentication context extracted from the RSTR token. (If the token is a SAML 2.0 assertion, the SAML-IdP/ICIM-SP can simply copy the saml:AuthenticationContext element from the token into a newly constructed assertion).

7. The user is logged-in to the SAML-SP.

A similar framework is used in the case of a WS-Federation-enabled SP. Further details of this integration framework, and examples of the framework messages, can be found at the Project Concordia web site[38].

A scheme for integrating CardSpace and Liberty has also been proposed by Jørstada, Thuan, Jønvike and Thanh [110]. This scheme requires the user to possess a mobile phone with Short Message Service (SMS) support. The concept is simple; the IdP must support both CardSpace and Liberty, so that a CS-E user agent will be able to access any SP supporting either Liberty or CardSpace, without requiring an identity management adapter to be installed on the user machine. Moreover, the IdP must perform the same user authentication technique, regardless of the identity management system the user is trying to use. The IdP simply sends an SMS to the user, and, in order to be authenticated, the user must confirm receiving that SMS.

---

[38]http://projectconcordia.org/index.php/Infocard_Authentication_Scenario_Details

This confirmation is also an implicit user approval for the IdP to send a security token (or assertion) to the SP.

4.8.2   Delegation

Providing support for delegation services (see Section 2.2.3) in an identity management system enhances its practicality by improving its flexibility and scalability. Delegation enables an SP to perform tasks on behalf of its users (e.g. obtaining user information from another SP in order to create a new user account). Delegation must be bound to user consent; i.e. an SP must obtain the consent of the user before performing a particular task on the user's behalf.

4.8.2.1   Shibboleth Delegation Framework

Draft specifications for a Shibboleth delegation system were published in 2005 [43]. More recently, in September 2008 an announcement[39] appeared on the Shibboleth web site stating that delegation support is on the Shibboleth development road map. At the time of writing, the 2005 drafts have not been superseded. Most recently, in November 2009 Shibboleth released a software plug-in[40] that can be installed with Shibboleth to support delegation for web portals; this plug-in conforms to the 2005 draft specifications.

The Shibboleth delegation framework is essentially a SAML authentication assertion delegation framework, and it can be built on either the Browser POST or the ECP SSO profile (see Section 2.4.2). Figure 4.22 provides a sketch of the Shibboleth delegation system message flows (for the Browser POST profile case).

---

[39]https://spaces.internet2.edu/display/SHIB2/Shibboleth+Roadmap
[40]https://spaces.internet2.edu/display/ShibuPortal/Configuring+Shibboleth+Delegation+for+a+Portal

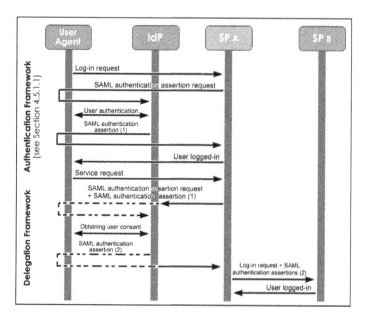

Figure 4.22: Shibboleth delegation framework (Browser POST)

As shown the figure, the authentication process described in Section 4.5.1.1 must be performed prior to performing the delegation procedure. The main steps in the delegation procedure are as follows.

1. The user is authenticated by an SP, A, using the authentication procedure described in Section 4.5.1.1. This results in A obtaining a SAML authentication assertion signed by the IdP. This assertion is referred to below as *assertion-1*.

2. Subsequently, suppose the user requests a service from A that requires certain user information to be obtained from another SP, B.

3. In order to obtain the required information, A must log-in to B on behalf of the user. This involves A sending a new SAML authentication assertion request to the IdP along with *assertion-1*. The inclusion of *assertion-1* proves

141

to the IdP that the user has recently accessed A. This message can be sent either by redirecting the user agent to the IdP web site, or directly from A to the IdP.

4. The IdP asks the user for her consent via the user agent.

5. After the user has provided her consent, the IdP checks the validity of *assertion-1*. If *assertion-1* is valid, then the IdP generates a new SAML authentication assertion to be presented to B (in which the subject is the user). This assertion is referred to below as *assertion-2*. The IdP then sends *assertion-2* to A either by redirecting the user agent to A's web site, or directly to A.

6. A then forwards *assertion-2* to B.

7. Finally, after checking the validity of *assertion-2*, B grants A access to the required information on behalf of the user.

The 2005 draft specification [43] recommends that the SAML proof-of-rightful-possession (or subject confirmation) method (see Section 3.3.4.3) specified within *assertion-2* is HoK; however, Bearer assertion can also be used. If the HoK method is used, the IdP must include the key information within *assertion-2*.

According to the model introduced in Chapter 2, this framework is not really a delegation framework; instead it is essentially a 'user-masquerading' framework, in which SPs are able to impersonate users, which raises a number of concerns regarding user accountability. Moreover, the framework does not offer a reliable means to ensure that the delegation assertion will be used for a specific privilege or role.

4.8.2.2 OAuth Delegation Framework

OAuth[41] is an open delegation framework designed to enable users to share private resources (e.g. photos, videos, contact lists, etc.) stored by one SP with another SP without having to reveal the security credentials associated with the first SP to the second. The OAuth 1.0 specifications were released in 2007 [16]; a revised version of these specifications was subsequently released in 2009 [75].

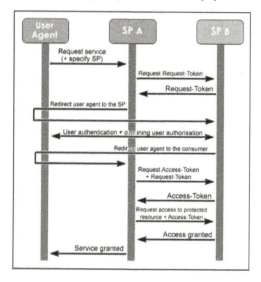

Figure 4.23: The OAuth delegation framework

Figure 4.23 provides a sketch of the OAuth framework message flows. Prior to execution of the framework, the two SPs involved must establish an identifier and a secret called a *consumer key* and a *consumer secret*, respectively. The main steps in the delegation framework are as follows (given that the exchanged messages in this framework are very short, we also provide examples of the main messages).

1. The user requests an SP, *A* say, via the user agent, to perform a task that requires certain information belongs to the user to be obtained from another SP, *B* say.

2. *A* first tries to access the necessary information stored on *B*'s server. However,

---
[41]http://oauth.net

we suppose that it receives an HTTP 401 error message, indicating that the required information is private and can not be accessed without authorisation.

3. *A* then sends an HTTP POST request message to *B* containing a 'Request-Token', which incorporates a random value that acts as a reference for the request. This message is MACed using the consumer key. The MAC is held in the signature field. An example of such a message is as follows.

```
https://SP-B.com/request_token?oauth_consumer_key=evb1234rd9
&oauth_signature_method=PLAINTEXT&oauth_signature=k93k4268kf54
&oauth_timestamp=31012010&oauth_nonce=8485hbf75b330
&oauth_version=1.0&oauth_callback=http://SP-A.com/token_request
```

4. After checking the validity of the MAC, *B* replies with a Request-Token message in the body of an HTTP response. An example of such a message is as follows.

```
oauth_token=ynk56vcck98&oauth_token_secret=kc244456ao03
&oauth_callback_confirmed=true
```

5. After receiving the Request-Token, *A* redirects the user agent to *B*, and attaches the received Request-Token to *B*'s URL, as in the following example.

```
http://SP-B.com/authorize?oauth_token=ynk56vcck98
```

6. *B* authenticates the user (e.g. using username and password). The user must be authenticated every time the framework is used. The authentication method by which *B* authenticates the user is beyond the scope of OAuth. After the user has successfully been authenticated, he/she is asked whether or not *A* should be granted access to the requested information.

7. If the user approves the request, *B* redirects the user agent back to *A* with a verification code attached to *A*'s URL, as in the following example.

```
http://SP-A.com/token_request?oauth_token=ynk56vcck98
&oauth_verifier=bgh758204nft
```

8. *A* then sends an HTTP POST request message to *B* to request an 'Access-Token', which can later be used to access the private resources stored by *B*. This message is also MACed using the consumer key. An example of such a message is as follows.

```
https://SP-B.com/access_token?oauth_consumer_key=evb1234rd9
&oauth_token=ynk56vcck98&oauth_signature_method=PLAINTEXT
&oauth_signature=k93k4268kf54hg67320ge4v
&oauth_timestamp=31012010&oauth_nonce=bvhgf657494932yfhbf
&oauth_version=1.0&oauth_verifier=bgh758204nft
```

9. After checking the validity of the MAC, *B* replies with an Access-Token in the message body of an HTTP response. An example of such a message is as follows.

```
oauth_token=rtra6456484j56&oauth_token_secret=pfnvbr4s0er
```

10. Finally, *A* presents the received Access-Token to *B*, and, after checking its validity, *B* grants *A* access to the requested information. The Access-Token can be used more than once within a single working session.

We observe that the OAuth delegation framework is simple and efficient; however, it has a number of security and practicality issues. One shortcoming is that most of the protocols used are proprietary (i.e. non-standardised). The framework would potentially be more reliable and interoperable if it was built on standardised protocols (e.g. SAML, SOAP, WS-*, etc.). Additionally, the framework does not support robust authentication means for a user to authenticate the SP (e.g. using high-assurance certificates) before giving it permission to access her/his private data. As discussed in Section 4.7.2, judging the reliability of an SP based on an SSL/TLS certificate (or weaker mechanisms) is risky, and leaves users open to attack from malicious SPs. Finally, we observe that the framework does not protect the user from being deceived by a malicious SP which redirects the user agent to a fake web site in order to steal the user's credentials.

4.8.2.3 Related Work

One of the most widely discussed techniques to support delegation in a web-based identity management system is to extend SAML attribute assertions to carry delegation information. Such techniques have been discussed by a number of authors (see, for example, Gomi et al. [72] and Wang, del Vecchio and Humphrey [176]). In these schemes, the IdP acts as a delegation authority, and SAML attribute statements are used by SPs as delegation assertions.

A number of other approaches to providing support for delegation via XML-based protocols have been discussed, including the grid delegation protocol of Ahsant, Basney and Mulmo [7], which is designed for grid applications and uses the WS-Trust protocol. Other examples include the approaches described in [49, 158, 163] which use XACML, and the Wohlgemuth-Müller scheme [182] which is built on proxy-based PKI services. Chadwick [46], proposes extensions to the X.509 [104] that can be used to implement a 'delegation issuing service'; this service issues X.509 attribute certificates on behalf of an attribute authority. These latter extensions are defined using Abstract Syntax Notation One (ASN.1) [105].

Finally, we mention the work of Austel et al. [17], who investigated the feasibility of using the CardSpace, Higgins, and OAuth frameworks to support delegation for Mashup[42] web sites. For CardSpace and Higgins they propose a 'user-masquerading' technique similar to that used in the Shibboleth delegation framework; this enables SPs to use security tokens issued to users by the IdP to access other SPs.

---

[42]http://en.wikipedia.org/wiki/Open_Mashup_Alliance

Part II

Enhancing Privacy and Practicality

CHAPTER 5

Enhancing user privacy in ICIM systems

Contents

This chapter proposes a method to enhance the privacy of ICIM systems by mitigating the risk of users being deceived by fake SPs. The scheme also reduces the risk of an attacker impersonating a legitimate user to access services offered by one or more

*SPs, after having broken the only means employed to authenticate the user to iden-
tity provider. This can be achieved by addressing two of the security vulnerabilities
outlined in Section 4.7, namely the reliance on user judgements of SP authenticity,
and the reliance on a single layer of authentication.*

*In this chapter CardSpace is used as an example of an ICIM system, and the modifi-
cation is described in the context of this system. The proposed approach is compatible
with the currently deployed CardSpace identity management system, and should enhance the privacy of this system whilst involving only minor changes to the current
CardSpace framework. We also provide a security and performance analysis of the
proposal. Other possible approaches addressing the outlined security shortcomings
are described at the end of the chapter. Much of the material in this chapter has
previously been published in [9, 12].*

5.1 Introduction

The growing use of Internet web applications gives rise to the problem of managing
the necessary digital identities and preserving their privacy. In an open large-scale
domain such as the Internet, preserving user privacy is not a straightforward task.
Identity theft, which occurs when an impostor uses a legitimate user's identifying
information without his/her consent, is becoming one of the biggest security concerns
both for users and for organisations offering services on the Internet.

In this chapter we focus on two particular security shortcomings of CardSpace,
namely its reliance on user judgements of SP authenticity, and its dependence on
a single layer of user authentication to the IdP (see Section 4.7). The scheme described in this chapter aims to mitigate the risk of users being deceived by fake
SPs (e.g. as might arise through phishing), and the risk of an attacker impersonat-

ing a legitimate user, after having broken the single authentication layer between the user and the IdP. This is achieved by means of a novel scheme based on the concept of Secured from Identity Theft (SIT) attributes [22] and on zero-knowledge cryptographic techniques (see Section 2.3.7).

The remainder of this chapter is organised as follows. In Section 5.2 we briefly discuss the security problems we aim to address, and we then propose a scheme which addresses them. In Section 5.3 a security and performance analysis of the novel scheme is given, in addition to a discussion of its possible limitations. In Section 5.4 other possible solutions are briefly discussed and, finally, Section 5.5 concludes the chapter.

5.2 Improving the Security of CardSpace

In Section 4.7, we outlined a number of security limitations that are shared by all the identity management systems discussed in Chapter 4 (including CardSpace). In this Section, we propose a scheme that addresses two of these limitations, namely the reliance on user judgements of SP authenticity, and the reliance on a single layer of authentication.

5.2.1 The Security Problems

In CardSpace, the user is responsible for judging the authenticity of the SP. This judgement is a security-critical task, because the SP may obtain personal information belonging to the user in the form of 'asserted claims' sent within a security token. Thus, if a malicious SP successfully impersonates a genuine SP, it could gather personal information about users, and potentially use this information in unauthorised ways. Accordingly, any misjudgement of the authenticity of an SP could result in a serious privacy violation. In general, it would appear that a typical user is not qualified to make such a security critical decision.

In Section 4.7 we discussed the three possible methods that can be used by an SP to prove its identity, namely using a high-assurance public key certificate, using an 'ordinary' public key certificate (e.g. an SSL/TLS certificate), or using no certificate at all. Many users do not pay much attention when they are asked to approve a digital certificate, either because they do not understand the importance of the approval decision, or because they know that they must approve the certificate in order to get access to a particular web site. SPs without any certificates at all can be used (given user consent), and this leads to a serious risk of a privacy violation. Even the warning provided by the Identity Selector when a user accesses an SP for the first time cannot completely solve this problem (as discussed in Section 4.7).

Moreover, in the case where a single IdP and multiple SPs are involved in a single working session, which seems likely to be a typical scenario, the security of CardSpace within that working session will rely on a single layer of authentication, i.e. the authentication of the user to the IdP. In the currently deployed version of CardSpace, this user authentication can be achieved using one of four methods, namely username/password, Kerberos V5 ticket, X.509 certificate, or self-issued SAML 1.1 assertion; however, it seems likely that, in many cases, a simple username/password authentication technique will be used. If a working session is hijacked (e.g. by compromising a Kerberos token), or the password is cracked (e.g. via guessing, brute-force, key logging, or dictionary attacks), then the security of the entire system will be compromised (again as discussed in Section 4.7).

Below we propose a scheme that addresses these two potential security issues. That is, the scheme aims to mitigate the risk of users being deceived by fake SPs (e.g. as might arise through phishing), and the risk of an attacker impersonating a legitimate user after having broken the single means used by the IdP to authenticate the user.

5.2.2 The Novel Scheme

The scheme we propose is based on the concept of Secured from Identity Theft (SIT) attributes [22]. The SIT scheme does not rely on a PKI, and was originally proposed for use for online user attribute registration with a trusted registrar. The SIT scheme is based on the Schnorr zero-knowledge protocol (see Section 2.3.7). In the novel scheme described here, CardSpace claims are treated as SIT attributes.

The scheme operates as follows. Instead of including the actual value of the claim in the security token in step 7 of the message flow illustrated in Section 4.2.1, the IdP includes data computed as a function of the claim. It must not be feasible for the CEUA or the SP to deduce the value of the claim using only this data. It merits mentioning here that the structure and the content of the security token will remain the same (e.g. including time-stamps, PPIDs, signature values, etc.), except the part that includes the actual value of the claim. We next examine the operation of the scheme in greater detail.

It is important to note that this scheme is not intended to replace the use of extended validation certificates. Such certificates, particularly if they include a readily recognisable item such as a corporate logo, are a potentially valuable way of improving user understanding of authentication issues. Similarly, the scheme is not intended to replace the warning provided by the CardSpace Identity Selector when a user accesses an SP for the first time, as these warnings are potentially useful and do not conflict with the scheme.

5.2.2.1   Protocol Requirements

Prior to use of the protocol, the IdP must select three domain parameters, p, q and g, where p and q are large primes satisfying $q|(p-1)$, and g is an element of multiplicative order q in $\mathbb{Z}_p^*$. These domain parameters must be made known to the CEUA and the SP in a reliable way, e.g. by inclusion in a certificate signed by a trusted CA. The IdP, CEUA and SP are all required to know the actual value of the claim prior to the protocol run, or at least know that it lies within a small set of possible values. Providing the SP with the claim value can be be achieved by requiring the user and the SP to conduct a registration procedure prior to use of the protocol, in which the user registers the claim values that can later be asserted to this particular SP. Similarly, the IdP is equipped with the value during user registration. We assume that the user provides the CEUA with the claim value (see also Sections 5.2.2.2 and 5.3.1.4).

The goal is to prevent the need to reveal the actual values of the claims to the SP or IdP during use of the CardSpace framework. This means that no party will have to trust any other party to the level that it has to reveal the actual values of the claims to it.

Finally, we assume that the IdP imposes an additional authentication procedure on the user if he/she wishes to retrieve, delete, or edit its attributes. As a result, if an attacker obtains the password used to authenticate the user to the IdP during framework execution, it cannot use this password to access the user attributes stored by the IdP.

5.2.2.2   Protocol Steps

The following protocol forms the basis of the proposed solution.

1. **IdP** → **CEUA** : $s = g^{-c} \bmod p$ [where c is the claim value, and s is included in a security token].

2. **CEUA** → **SP** : $s, d = g^r \bmod p$ [where r is a random integer $(1 \leqslant r \leqslant q-1)$ chosen by the CEUA].

3. **SP** → **CEUA** : e [e is a random integer $(1 \leqslant e \leqslant 2^t)$ chosen by the RP, and t is a security parameter].

4. **CEUA** → **SP** : $y = r + ec \bmod q$

5. **SP**: if $d = g^y s^e \bmod p$, then user authentication is successful.

All the messages sent in the above protocol must be conveyed over a channel that protects both confidentiality and integrity (e.g. an SSL/TLS channel). The protocol can easily be integrated into the currently deployed CardSpace framework; indeed, no changes to the framework are required. However, some minor changes must be made to the way that each party handles the security tokens. Steps 1, 2 and 5 of the above protocol should be integrated with steps 7, 8 and 9, respectively, of the message flow described in section 4.2.1. The value s should be digitally signed by the IdP by including it within the security token (e.g. using an XML-signature within a SAML assertion).

After the second step of the protocol above, the SP knows that the IdP is asserting a claim from the inclusion of $s = g^{-c} \bmod p$ in the token; if, moreover, the SP knows in advance the expected value of c, then it can use the received value s to verify whether the IdP is asserting this expected value or not. Also, if the SP knows that c lies within a certain small set of values, then the SP can determine which is being asserted by a simple trial and error process; however, if the set of possible values for c is very large, then the SP does not learn anything about the asserted claim. After the protocol has completed, and if user authentication is successful, then the SP can grant the requested service to the user. Not only does successful completion of the protocol mean that the IdP is asserting the claim regarding the user, but it also proves that the user knows the claim value c, providing an additional layer of user authentication. Of course, the strength of this additional layer of authentication will depend on whether the claim is readily guessable by a third party.

Note that, (as stated in Section 5.2.2.1) prior to step 4 of the protocol, the user must pass the CEUA the values of the attributes being asserted, i.e. the CEUA must be given sufficient information to obtain c. This could, for example, involve the CEUA creating a dialogue box for the user to complete. This has implications for the usability of the scheme, and alternative means for the CEUA to obtain c are discussed in section 5.3.1.4 below.

The protocol thus enables the IdP to assert a claim about a user, and for the user to confirm knowledge of this claim, without revealing the claim to the SP. This means that the user does not need to trust an SP not to misuse a revealed claim. Also, the scheme has the advantage that it does not require any additional key management.

In the case of self-issued tokens, The SIP must include in the InfoCard the value $s = g^{-c} \bmod p$ instead of the actual value of the claim.

The above scheme is based on a specific cryptosystem, namely the Schnorr protocol. It would be possible to replace this scheme with any other scheme with similar properties. More specifically, we require a protocol which enables both the CEUA and the SP to prove knowledge of the claim c, so that the SP knows that they both know the claim, but with the property that c is not revealed in this process. The particular advantage of the Schnorr scheme in this context is that it achieves these objectives in an efficient way, and can be seamlessly incorporated into the CardSpace message flows.

5.3 Analysis

We now provide a security and performance analysis of the scheme.

5.3.1 Security

We first consider the scheme's security properties.

5.3.1.1 Addressing the Limitations

As we now demonstrate, the scheme proposed in section 5.2 addresses both of the highlighted security limitations.

The scheme avoids the need to rely on the user's judgement of the trustworthiness of the SP by avoiding the need for trust between the user and the SP. In the revised protocol the user does not reveal any personal information to the SP; instead, the user demonstrates knowledge of this information. Of course, the user will still have to trust the SP at least once in order to register her/his personal information with this SP (e.g. when he/she first registers with that SP), and this trust is likely to be based on a public key certificate (e.g. the SP's SSL certificate). However, it appears reasonable to assume that the user will be more careful during this one-off registration procedure than in routine use of the SP service.

The modified protocol no longer relies on a single layer of authentication. If the working session is hijacked (e.g. by compromising a Kerberos token), or the user's password is cracked, then the security of the system will not be totally breached, since the solution adds a new layer of authentication. When trying to log-in to an SP, an attacker will not be able to demonstrate knowledge of the user's personal

156

information, and hence the SP will not let the attacker log in. Moreover, the attacker cannot learn the user's personal information, since the claim values will not be included in the security token.

5.3.1.2 Privacy

The scheme increases the level of privacy provided to CardSpace users since, as described in section 5.2, claim values are not revealed at any stage (except during registration). This is a significant enhancement to the privacy protection offered by CardSpace. Additionally, unlike in the currently deployed CardSpace identity framework (under the default settings), the user does not have to reveal the identity of the SP to the IdP. This should also enhance user privacy.

The scheme implicitly assumes that it will not be possible to recover c from knowledge of $g^{-c} \bmod p$, where g and p are publicly known. Assuming that the Discrete Logarithm Problem [122] is difficult with respect to g in the multiplicative group of integers modulo p, this can be guaranteed by requiring the number of possible values for c to be sufficiently large, e.g. at least 2^{128}. Clearly, not all claim types have such a large number of possible values; possible solutions to this guessing problem are discussed in Section 5.3.1.3 below.

The proposed scheme satisfies the requirements of the second law of Microsoft's own laws of identity to a greater degree than the currently deployed CardSpace framework, where this law states that only the minimum amount of identifying information should be revealed (see Section 4.1). Similarly, the scheme satisfies the requirements of the first principle of the OECD's principles for personal data protection to a greater degree than CardSpace (see Section 2.2.7.2).

5.3.1.3   The Guessing Problem

As discussed above, since the scheme is based on disguising user personal informa-tion, there is always the risk of an attacker guessing this information, thus breaking the user authentication means provided by the scheme.

Some claims can be easily guessed, especially in the case of 'user-oriented' attacks where information about the user is already known by the attacker. Examples of such claims include first name, home country, age, and marital status. If an attacker successfully broke the CardSpace first layer of authentication (which might, for example, be password-based), then she/he could try to guess a particular claim and verify whether or not her/his guess is correct before forwarding the security token to the SP. This can be done using the publicly known parameters p and g and the value s received in step 1 of the protocol run.

We propose two possible ways of addressing this problem:

- The first, which has certain advantages, requires the SP to choose 'hard-to-guess' claims to be asserted by the IdP, such as a combination of a series of attributes which are collectively hard-to-guess, e.g. a combination of mother's maiden name, social security number and credit card number. The SP also has an incentive to follow such a strategy, since a successful guessing attack, if combined with breaking the first level of authentication, would allow an imposter user to log in to an SP. Indeed, many SPs already rely on 'hard-to-guess' personal information to authenticate users when they forget their passwords. Such an approach can also help the user mitigate the risk of a fake SP guessing the personal information of the user and verifying the correctness of its guesses using the publicly known parameters and the value s. Observe that this requires the SP to know the amount of entropy associated with each claim value, which may not always be the case. However, it seems reasonable to assume that in most cases the SP can make a rough estimate which is unlikely to be wildly inaccurate.

This approach can be reinforced by requiring the Identity Selector to refuse to request an assertion for claims that have insufficient entropy. For example, the Identity Selector could keep an indication of the approximate number of bits of entropy associated with each claim, so that it can add the values for the requested claims to obtain an estimate for the total entropy for the requested set of claims before deciding whether or not to make a request for an assertion. Such a process also protects against the situation where the SP makes a highly inaccurate assessment of the entropy of the collection of attribute values it is requesting.

A limitation of this approach is that it assumes that the IdP is the source of authority for multiple hard-to-guess claims which might not be the normal case.

- Another approach would be for the IdP to mask the claim value, e.g. by using the value $c + x$ instead of c, where x is a random value selected by the IdP and shared with the user prior to the protocol run (we assume that x cannot be retrieved using the user security credentials employed by the IdP during use of CardSpace). The means by which the session-specific random value x is agreed by the CEUA and the IdP is clearly critical to the security of the scheme. One possibility would be for the CEUA and the IdP to conduct a Diffie-Hellman key exchange (see section 2.4.4) to agree the value of x. Alternatively, x could be sent as a parameter in the message to the CEUA, although it would be prone to interception on this link (noting that it would not be sent in clear-text across the CEUA-SP link). The value of x can then be shared with the SP by encrypting it using the SP public key and inserting it into the security token. This will prevent the attacker from impersonating the legitimate user even if it can guess the claim value, since it does not know the value of x. However, this solution requires the user to reveal the identity of the SP to the IdP, and this removes one of the advantages of the scheme (as discussed in Section 5.3.1.2). Since x is made available to the SP, its use does not protect against claim-guessing by the SP.

5.3.1.4 Access to Claims by the CEUA

The scheme requires the CEUA to be aware of the actual value of the claim in order to generate a response to the challenge message it receives from the SP. In some cases it is not realistic to expect users to memorise all their registered claim values, so that they can pass them to the CEUA when required. Certain claims can be hard to remember, such as a health record number or a credit card number. Moreover, being required to enter the actual values of the claims every time a user logs in to a web site might be extremely inconvenient. Hence we consider other means by which the CEUA might retrieve the actual values of the claims.

We propose four approaches, although each has certain limitations, and access to claim values by the CEUA remains a key problem:

1. *Storing the claim values on a trusted server*: users could retrieve their registered claim values from a third party server (after being authenticated by the server). However, this would add complexity to the framework.

2. *Storing the claim values on a hardware user token*: Such an approach is potentially more reliable and less complex than the first approach. Storing the claims on a hardware token, such as USB memory stick or smart card, would add an authentication factor to the scheme (i.e the possession of the token). This solution is similar to currently used ID card identification processes, where

160

a person needs to present an identification card in order to be authenticated. However, token provisioning and management adds significant user complexity.

3. *Retrieving the claim values directly from the IdP by the CEUA*: the user could request the IdP to provide it with the claim values, after the IdP has authenticated the user using security credentials distinct from those used during the CardSpace framework. Such a process would have to take place outside the current CardSpace framework. Also, it would mean adding one more message to the framework.

4. *Storing the claim values in the identity selector*. CardSpace itself could store the claim values in encrypted form, as is the case for claim values corresponding to self-issued cards. Note that the claim values for self-issued cards are not stored in the cards themselves, but by the SIP, an approach that could also be followed here.

5.3.1.5   Use of SIT attributes

The proposed scheme requires the SP to know the values of the asserted attributes in advance, or, at least, to know that they lie within a certain small set of values. However, some attributes may have a huge set of possible values. In order to solve this problem an SP could, for example, link specific attribute values to a local user identifier (e.g. by requiring the user to submit them in a registration phase). Subsequently, when the user tries to log-in to that SP, it would ask the user to provide her/his local identifier before using CardSpace. Such an identifier could be stored in the form of an HTTP cookie for user convenience. This solution could adversely affect the usability of CardSpace since many CardSpace-enabled SPs do not require attribute-registration.

However, it could be argued that, since the SP already knows the values of the attributes, all that is required is for the IdP to assert that a user with a particular identity (or pseudonym) has been authenticated. This would greatly simplify the scheme as presented. However, such a simplification would mean the loss of a number of valuable properties of the proposed scheme, including the following.

- First, the scheme provides evidence to the SP that the user knows the values of the attributes, i.e. that the user knows c, and hence functions as an additional means of user authentication.

- Second, the SP might wish to know that the attribute values it possesses are still valid and/or correct. For example it might have the user's Credit Card number, but it might wish to have an assertion from the IdP (which might be the issuing bank) that this number is still the number associated with the user.

- Third, the SP does not, in fact, need to know the precise value of the claim c. It could be that the IdP asserts one of a small number of different claim values for the user, depending on the context. The precise claim value being asserted can be discovered by the SP via an exhaustive search.

5.3.2 Performance

The proposed scheme can readily be integrated into the currently deployed CardSpace framework. Only two steps need to be added to the framework described in Section 4.2; these two steps involve exchanging the zero-knowledge-proof messages, and should take place at the end of the message flow. An additional step may be needed if the third proposed solution to the problem of retrieving the claim values by the CEUA is adopted (as described in section 5.3.1.4).

Incorporating the protocol into the CardSpace message flow requires some minor changes to the contents of the security token. Other than these changes, the meta-system remains precisely the same (including the security token format, message flow, etc.). Table 5.1 shows the computational load imposed by the scheme on each system party, where E_f denotes a modular exponentiation with respect to a fixed base, M denotes a modular multiplication, and E_v denotes a modular exponentiation to a variable base. Addition and comparison operations have been neglected in these assessments of computational load because their complexity is much less than that of the exponentiation and multiplication operations.

Table 5.1: Computational load on system parties

Party	Computational load
IdP	$1E_f$
CEUA	$1E_f + 1M$
SP	$1E_f + 1E_v + 1M$

From Table 5.1 we conclude that the scheme imposes a manageable computational load on the involved parties, given that modular exponentiations can be performed in milliseconds on modern processors [144].

The shared parameters p, q and g can be changed frequently if required, and the task of deploying these shared parameters could be achieved using one of a number of simple methods, e.g. by publishing these parameters on the IdP web site. The proposed scheme has the advantage that it does not require any additional key management.

5.3.3 Limitations

One limitation of the scheme is that it requires the IdP to use two different means to authenticate the user, in order to create two authentication layers. One is employed to authenticate the user when managing the attributes stored by the IdP, and the other is employed during CardSpace operation before the IdP forwards the requested security token to the user. This might place an additional burden on the user; however, if one of the methods described in Sections 5.4.1 and 5.4.2 below is used, then this assumption can be dropped.

Another limitation is that the proposed scheme does not support the use of a one-time claim (e.g. a credit card one-time code). As stated earlier in this chapter, prior to the protocol run the SP must know the actual value of the claim that it requests the IdP to assert, or at least it must know that the claim value lies within a certain small set of values.

Finally note that the actual value of the claim is not included in the security token but has to be either known and stored by the CEUA, or entered by the user each time. As pointed out in Section 5.3.1.4, the proposed solutions to this problem all have certain limitations. Resolving this issue is therefore critical for the practical use of the SIT-based scheme for CardSpace.

5.4 Other possible solutions

We now consider three further ways in which the two highlighted privacy issues might be addressed. Two of these approaches can be combined with the scheme described in Section 5.2, whereas the other is an alternative.

5.4.1 Using Symmetric Proof-keys

The reliance on a single layer of authentication could be addressed by using a long-term secret shared by the IdP and a user. Such a secret could be exploited to provide a second layer of user authentication in a variety of ways; in this section and in Section 5.4.2 we consider two approaches of this type. Both involve making use of the CardSpace proof-key.

The first approach requires a slight modification to the *symmetric* proof-of-rightful-possession method outlined in Section 3.3.4.2. The IdP and the user must first establish a long-term shared secret (k_1), e.g. at the time of user registration with the IdP. This secret could, for example, be generated by the IdP and stored on the user machine or a portable user token (e.g. a USB memory stick or smart card). In order to change this secret (or be re-issued with it), the user would need to conduct a secure exchange with the IdP. To avoid the need to store the secret key on the user machine or a token, it could be derived from a user-memorised password, e.g. by applying a cryptographic hash-function to the password and truncating the result appropriately.

If the *symmetric* proof-of-rightful-possession method is used, the CardSpace IdP includes a short-term secret (k_2) in the security token, asymmetrically encrypted using the SP's public key. We propose that the IdP instead includes an asymmetrically encrypted version of the value $f = h(k_1 || k_2)$, where k_2 is a short term secret, h is a cryptographic hash function, and $||$ denotes concatenation of bit strings. The value f is encrypted using the SP's public key, just as in the 'standard' scheme, and the IdP sends the short term secret k_2 to the user, again as in the standard scheme.

The CEUA can now re-compute the value f (using the user stored value of k_1 and the received value of k_2) to prove its rightful possession of the security token. Since this value is computed using the long-term secret k_1, this process adds an additional layer of authentication. That is, if the first layer of authentication between the IdP and the user is broken (e.g. if the password is compromised), then the attacker will still need to know the long-term secret in order to access the services offered by the

SP. This scheme can readily be integrated into CardSpace.

5.4.2   Using Asymmetric Proof-keys

A second way of using a long-term secret shared by the user and an IdP to pro-vide a second layer of user authentication involves making a small modification to the *asymmetric* proof-of-rightful-possession method, outlined in Section 3.3.4.2. We present the scheme in the context of a discrete logarithm based asymmetric cryp-tosystem, although variants for other types of asymmetric cryptosystem may well be possible.

Suppose the user and IdP have agreed on the use of a finite cyclic group G of (large) order q, and a generator g of G, where finding discrete logarithms for elements of G with respect to the base g is computationally infeasible. Suppose also that the user and IdP share a secret integer k (where $0 < k < q$). Then, when requesting a token from the IdP, the user generates a random integer x (where $0 < x < q$), and sends g^x to the IdP instead of sending its public key, as would normally be the case for use of an asymmetric proof-key. The user computes and retains ($xk \bmod q$) as its private proof-key. The IdP then computes $g^{xk}(= (g^x)^k)$, and includes this in the token as the asymmetric proof-key public key.

The remainder of the operation of the scheme is then identical to that for the 'stan-dard' asymmetric proof-key scheme. That is, the CEUA possesses a private key corresponding to the public key in the token. The CEUA can then use this private key to prove ownership of the token.

5.4.3   Modifying Claim Requests

Another way of addressing the problem of fake SPs avoids the need for the SP to request sensitive information in the security token provided by the IdP. By doing so, the security token then becomes much less privacy sensitive, and hence providing such a token to an fake SP is no longer a major issue. That is, instead of seeking to avoid providing tokens to fake SPs, we attempt to minimise the privacy sensitivity of tokens.

Such an approach requires the SP to know the user information in advance (as is the case for the solution discussed in section 5.2). We exploit this knowledge by modifying the form of the request provided by the SP. That is, instead of asking for user personal information, the SP asks for the IdP to confirm that specific statements about the user's personal information are correct.

The IdP checks the information provided in the request and, if it is all correct, the IdP responds with a token asserting this fact. Such a token is clearly relatively non-sensitive.

Of course, this means that user information might be divulged to someone impersonating a user, since the SP submits its request for a token (which now contains potentially sensitive user information) before the user has been authenticated. It would appear difficult to address this issue without making minor modifications to the framework. For example, since the SP can inform the Identity Selector that the requested security token must be generated by a specific IdP, it could also encrypt its request so that only the specified IdP could read it. The Identity Selector could then forward the request to the IdP in its encrypted form.

5.4.4 Combining Solutions

To conclude, we briefly consider how the various solutions we have proposed might be combined. Firstly, it appears that the solutions proposed in 5.4.1 and 5.4.2 could readily be combined with the SIT-based solution proposed in Section 5.2. Indeed, using one of the solutions in 5.4.1 and 5.4.2 would allow dropping the assumption within the scheme described in 5.2 that the IdP must impose two different authentication procedures on the user, as these solutions provide a second layer of authentication.

By contrast, the idea briefly discussed in 5.4.3, i.e. where the SP requests confirmation of specified attributes instead of asking for the attribute values, should be seen as an alternative to the SIT-based scheme in section 5.2, rather than something that complements it. Of course, the scheme in Section 5.4.3 could easily be combined with the schemes in Sections 5.4.1 and 5.4.2, since they address completely different parts of the framework.

5.5 Conclusions

In this chapter we have proposed a modification to CardSpace that addresses two security limitations, namely its reliance on a user judgement of the authenticity of the SP, and its reliance on a single layer of authentication. The proposal involves applying Secured from Identity Theft (SIT) attributes, based on the Schnorr zero-knowledge protocol, to CardSpace. The scheme may be vulnerable to guessing attacks; however, we have also proposed a variety of measures to mitigate the risk of such attacks. The scheme has a number of other limitations. Most serious of these is the need for the CEUA to have access to the user claim values. A range of solutions to this issue have been proposed, they although all have certain limitations; as a result, we must conclude that resolving this issue is key to the practical implementation of the SIT-based scheme.

The proposed solution can readily be integrated into the currently deployed version of CardSpace identity management system; it can also be applied to other ICIM systems with similar message flows. Only two (or three) steps need to be added to the framework. The proposed solution requires some minor changes to the content of the security token issued by the IdP, and the involved parties only need to perform a small number of inexpensive computations.

Finally, we discussed other possible ways of addressing the two identified security limitations. Two of these approaches are based on the use of the proof-of-rightful-possession methods supported by CardSpace.

CHAPTER 6

Enhancing user authentication in ICIM systems

Contents

In ICIM systems, users identify themselves using security tokens that contain PII, and that are signed by an identity provider. However, a malicious IdP could readily impersonate any user by generating appropriate tokens. The growing number of identity theft techniques raises the risk of SPs being deceived by untrustworthy IdPs. We show how this vulnerability can be mitigated by adding an authentication layer between the user and the SP.

We propose two possible implementations of this layer. The first requires a user to perform an additional step before the SP completes the authentication process.

That is, the user must present to the SP certain information sent to the user by the SP during the most recent successful use of the scheme. A proof-of-concept implementation of this scheme has been produced. The second approach involves a challenge-response exchange between the user and the SP. This requires a minor modification to the service provider XML-based security policy declaration message. Much of the material in this chapter has previously been published in [13].

6.1   Introduction

In this chapter we focus on a vulnerability shared by all ICIM systems, namely the reliance on a single layer of authentication between the user and the IdP. We suggest that it would be of value to enhance user authentication in ICIM systems by adding an additional layer of authentication between the user and the SP. This is likely to be particularly useful since the SP is not provided with any evidence other than that provided by the IdP that a log-in attempt has been initiated by the legitimate user.

In this chapter we propose two possible methods to enhance user authentication. These methods give the SP an implicit indication that a log-in attempt has been initiated by the legitimate user. In the first method, a user must present to an SP certain information obtained during the last interaction with that SP. The second approach involves a challenge-response procedure between the user and the service provider, requiring a minor modification to the service provider XML-based security policy declaration message. This approach also gives the SP an indication of the involvement of the user in the log-in request.

The remainder of this chapter is organised as follows. Section 6.2 briefly discusses the importance of enhancing user authentication in ICIM systems. In Section 6.3

we propose two user authentication enhancing methods. In Section 6.4 we describe a prototype implementation of one of the methods. Section 6.5 discuss the effectiveness of the proposed methods, and Section 6.6 outlines certain of their limitations. Finally, Section 6.7 concludes the chapter.

6.2 User Authentication in ICIM Systems

In current ICIM systems, SPs are not provided with any user-originated evidence that the genuine user actually wishes to log in. Instead, SPs are given an IdP generated security token together with evidence of the user's rightful possession of this token, i.e. evidence that the user who forwarded the security token has the right to possess it. However, all the implemented proof-of-rightful-possession methods are based on information included within the security token itself (see Section 3.3.4.2). Moreover, the only means for the SP to judge the validity of a security token is by verifying the IdP's digital signature. This means that, if the identity provider is lying, then the 'proof-of-rightful-possession' could also be fabricated by the IdP.

We therefore propose the inclusion of an additional layer of authentication between the user and the SP, so that the SP does not rely completely on the single authentication layer between the user and the IdP (as in the current specifications of ICIM systems).

As discussed in Section 4.1, the first Law of Identity requires the provision of a high degree of 'user control and consent'; we therefore suggest that support for user consent in systems that adhere to these laws, such as CardSpace, needs to be enhanced so that the SP is provided with evidence of user consent. Also, there is a potential vulnerability because of the current lack of robust user-originated evidence.

Before proceeding we note that the problem we describe is less significant for self-issued InfoCards.

6.3 Enhancing User Authentication in ICIM Systems

In this section we propose two methods for enhancing user authentication in ICIM systems, both of which involve adding an additional layer of authentication between the user and the SP. The proposed methods are independent, and can be combined if desired. We describe the techniques as they apply to CardSpace; however, it would appear that they could also be applied to other ICIM systems.

6.3.1 A Proof-of-Authenticity Method

We now describe an approach to the provision of 'proof of authenticity' that requires the user platform to store a secret *proof-of-authenticity* value (known only to the client and the SP), that is sent to the SP during the authentication process. Provision of this secret value proves to the SP that the genuine user is involved. This adds an additional layer of authentication between the user and the SP.

The *proof-of-authenticity* value is randomly generated by the SP, and a new value is sent to the user platform after every successful authentication (e.g. in the form of an HTTP cookie). That is, when a user inaugurates a log-in procedure using the ICIM system, the SP will request the current *proof-of-authenticity* value from the user platform. The SP will verify that the provided value is as expected and, if so, will continue with the authentication process of the ICIM system. If a value is not available to the user platform (e.g. because this is the first occasion that the system has been used from this platform), or the provided value is incorrect (e.g. because the user has switched platforms), then the ICIM system authentication procedure will be aborted; the user will then be requested to authenticate him/herself by some other means (e.g. username and password). This latter means must involve the use of information not known to the IdP. Once the user has been authenticated (using the ICIM system or by some other means), the SP will generate a new random *proof-of-authenticity* value, store it, and send it to the user via a secure channel. This method assumes that the user always uses the same machine or has a portable hardware token (e.g. a smart card) on which to store the *proof-of-authenticity* value.

The provision of the *proof-of-authenticity* value should be transparent to the user, and hence will not affect the usability of the system. To demonstrate this fact, a prototype implementation of this scheme has been developed (see Section 6.4 below).

6.3.2   A Challenge-Response Method

This method requires the user platform to either share a secret key with the SP or possess a signature key pair for which the SP has a trusted copy of the public key. The key is used as the basis of a challenge-response authentication of the user to the SP, adding a new authentication layer between the user and the SP.

The proposed solution requires modifying the XML-based security policy declaration message sent from the SP to the user platform (i.e. to the Identity Selector) during security policy negotiation (see Section 3.3.4.2). Apart from presenting the requested token, the user platform is required to provide a valid response to a challenge sent by the SP. This response is computed using either a secret key shared by the user and the SP, or a private signature key belonging to the user. This method assumes that the user always uses the same machine or has a portable hardware token (e.g. a smart card) on which to store the key value.

6.3 Enhancing User Authentication in ICIM Systems

We now describe the operation of these two possibilities in greater detail.

6.3.2.1 MACed-response Mechanism

This mechanism requires the SP and the user to share a secret key. This key can be issued by the SP during the registration phase (i.e. when the user first registers an account with the SP). It can be replaced if lost or compromised, and can be stored on the user machine or on a security token such as a smartcard. Use of this mechanism also requires the SP and the user platform to agree on the use of a Message Authentication Code (MAC) algorithm, where we write $MAC_k(x)$ to denote a MAC computed on data x using the key k. We assume that the user establishes the shared secret key with the SP before any attempt at user impersonation by a malicious IdP.

In order to use this mechanism, the SP must have the ability to request a 'user-participation' assertion, which asserts that the legitimate user is the user participating in the current working session. This request can be embedded within its security policy declaration message. This requires certain minor modifications to be made to the WS-SecurityPolicy message that contains the SP security policy. To achieve this we propose the introduction of a new tag. This new XML tag, which we call <UserParticipation>, contains three data fields. The first holds the mechanism to be used, the second holds a boolean value that indicates whether or not the SP requires a user-participation assertion, and the third holds the challenge value (as explained below).

Figure 6.2 shows an *XML Schema* for the added tags. A *Document Type Definition* (DTD) for the new tag type is as shown in Figure 6.1.

Figure 6.3 gives an example of an XML message declaring an SP security policy ex-

175

```
<!ELEMENT UserParticipation (Type, AssertionRequested, Challenge)>

<!ELEMENT Type EMPTY>

<!ATTLIST Type Mechanism (MACed | Signed) "MACed">

<!ELEMENT AssertionRequested EMPTY>

<!ATTLIST AssertionRequested Enhanced (true | false) "false">

<!ELEMENT Challenge (#PCDATA)>
```

Figure 6.1: DTD for the new tags

pressed using the WS-SecurityPolicy standard (see Section 2.4.3). The policy states that the security token to be received must be issued by a specific IdP (*contoso.com*), and that the desired proof-of-rightful-possession method is the *Symmetric* method (see Section 3.3.4.2). The policy also lists the claims to be asserted (i.e. by listing their types in the security token). The requested claims are the given name and the surname, and each claim is defined using a specific URI. The novel tags are marked by inclusion within a box.

After processing the security policy of the SP, the Identity Selector on the user machine checks whether or not the SP is requesting a user-participation assertion by checking the value of the `<AssertionRequested>` field. If the value is *true*, then the Identity Selector extracts the value of the `<Challenge>` field, which is essentially a randomly generated *nonce* (i.e. a Number used ONCE). The CEUA then uses this nonce to generate the MAC value:

$$MAC_k(id_{SP}\|n)$$

where $\|$ denotes concatenation; id_{SP} is a reference for the SP, which could be the SP's domain name; n represents the received nonce; and k is the shared key.

The generated response is then sent to the SP along with the security token. Finally, the SP checks the response using the shared key k. If the MACed-response is correct,

176

```
<xs:schema xmlns:xs="http://www.w3.org/2001/XMLSchema"
elementFormDefault="qualified">
 <xs:import namespace="http://www.w3.org/XML/1998/namespace"/>
 <xs:element name="UserParticipation">
   <xs:complexType>
     <xs:sequence>
       <xs:element ref="Type"/>
       <xs:element ref="AssertionRequested"/>
       <xs:element ref="Challenge"/>
     </xs:sequence>
   </xs:complexType>
 </xs:element>
   <xs:element name="Type">
    <xs:complexType mixed="true">
   <xs:any minOccurs="0" maxOccurs="unbounded"
      namespace="##any" processContents="lax">
    <xs:annotation>
      <xs:documentation>
         Any xml content is allowed in this element.
      </xs:documentation>
    </xs:annotation>
   </xs:any>
       <xs:attribute name="Mechanism" default="MACed">
         <xs:simpleType>
           <xs:restriction>
             <xs:enumeration value="MACed"/>
             <xs:enumeration value="Signed"/>
           </xs:restriction>
         </xs:simpleType>
       </xs:attribute>
     </xs:complexType>
   </xs:element>
   <xs:element name="AssertionRequested"/>
     <xs:complexType mixed="true">
   <xs:any minOccurs="0" maxOccurs="unbounded"
      namespace="##any" processContents="lax">
    <xs:annotation>
      <xs:documentation>
         Any xml content is allowed in this element.
      </xs:documentation>
    </xs:annotation>
   </xs:any>
       <xs:attribute name="Enhanced" type="xs:boolean"
         default="false">
       </xs:attribute>
     </xs:complexType>
   </xs:element>
   <xs:element name="Challenge" type="xs:string "/>
 </xs:schema>
```

Figure 6.2: XML schema for the new tags

then this acts as an implicit indication that the log-in attempt was initiated by the legitimate user. The use of a nonce as a challenge helps to prevent replay attacks.

6.3.2.2 Signed-response Mechanism

In order to use this mechanism, the user platform must have access to a key pair for a digital signature scheme. The user and the SP must also agree on the use of a particular such scheme; we write $S_{user}(x)$ to denote the user signature on data

```
<sp:IssuedToken sp:Usage="xs:anyURI" sp:IncludeToken="xs:anyURI" ...>

   <sp:Issuer>
        <wsa:Address>
                http://contoso.com/sts
        </wsa:Address>
        <wsa:Metadata>
                ...
        </wsa:Metadata>
   </sp:Issuer>
    <sp:RequestSecurityTokenTemplate>
        <wst:KeyType>
                http://schemas.xmlsoap.org/ws/2005/02/trust/SymmetricKey
        </wst:KeyType>
        <wst:Claims Dialect="http://schemas.xmlsoap.org/ws/2005/05/identity">
        <ic:ClaimType Uri="http://.../ws/2005/05/identity/claims/givenname"/>
        <ic:ClaimType Uri="http://.../ws/2005/05/identity/claims/surname"
        Optional="true" />
        </wst:Claims>
    </sp:RequestSecurityTokenTemplate>
<wsp:Policy>
    <UserParticipation>
        <Type Mechanism="MACed">
            ... Related data can be placed here ...
        </Type>
        <AssertionRequested Enhanced="true">
            ... Related data can be placed here ...
        </AssertionRequested>
        <Challenge>
            ... Challenge value ...
        </Challenge>
    </UserParticipation>
    ...
    </wsp:Policy>
    ...
</sp:IssuedToken>
```

Figure 6.3: Modified SP security policy

x. The key pair can be issued to the user either by the SP during the registration phase (i.e. when the user first registers an account with the SP), or by a trusted CA (see Section 2.5). Of course, in the latter case the user must register its public key certificate with the SP before this mechanism can be used. The key pair can be replaced if lost or compromised, and can be stored on the user machine or on a security token such as a smartcard.

An obvious question would be: Why use CardSpace if there is already a PKI in use? The answer is simple: because the user and/or the SP might wish to use CardSpace to retrieve attributes from the IdP for authorisation purposes.

This mechanism works in exactly same way as the MACed-response mechanism,

178

except that instead of MACing the challenge value, the user platform signs the value using its private key. The value of the <Mechanism> field must be Signed. The response is the signature:

$$S_{user}(id_{SP}\|n)$$

where id_{SP} is a reference for the SP, which could be the SP's domain name; and n represents the received nonce.

6.4 Implementing the Proof-of-Authenticity Method

A proof of concept implementation of the proof-of-authenticity method has been successfully tested. The prototype was built on the Pamela Project's[1] implementation of the SP CardSpace component. The implementation involved modifying the component by creating two software modules to be held on the SP server; the two modules were written using the PHP programming language (version 5). The implementation has been successfully tested on an Apache web server (version 2.2.8) running on the Linux-Fedora operating system.

The *proof-of-authenticity* (*PoA*) is stored on the user machine in the form of an HTTP cookie. The *PoA* value is generated by hashing a combination of an SP-generated random value and transaction-specific information, to minimise the possibility of accidental re-use of the same value.

The two software modules that perform the required operations for the proof-of-authenticity method are called *PoASet* and *PoACheck*. These two modules are integrated with the CardSpace-enabling software on the SP's server. *PoASet* oper-

---

[1]http://pamelaproject.com/

ates once the user has been authenticated using a mechanism that does not rely on information known by the identity provider (e.g. using username/password). *PoASet* creates a *PoA*, stores it in a server database, and sends it to the user in the form of an HTTP cookie. *PoACheck* decides whether or not the user can use the CardSpace authentication system. It first checks whether or not the *PoA* provided by the user platform is valid. If not, then *PoACheck* denies the user request to use the CardSpace system, and informs the user that he/she will need to be authenticated using another mechanism. If the supplied *PoA* is correct, *PoACheck* creates a new *PoA*, stores it in its database, and sends a copy of it to the user in the form of an HTTP cookie. Finally, it redirects the user's browser to a web page where the user can perform the authentication process using the CardSpace framework[2].

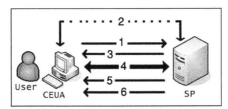

Figure 6.4: Initial login using the proof-of-authenticity method

Figure 6.4 shows the message flow for the first user login (i.e. where the user does not have a correct *PoA*). The message flow steps are as follows.

1. **CEUA → SP** : Login request using CardSpace.

2. **CEUA ↔ SP** : SP checks whether or not the user has got the correct *PoA*.

3. **CEUA ← SP** : Sorry you cannot use CardSpace this time!

4. **CEUA ↔ SP** : Authentication of the user using another mechanism (e.g. username/password).

5. **CEUA ← SP** : You have been authenticated. Welcome!

---

[2]The source code of the two modules is given in an appendix to this thesis.

6. **CEUA** ← **SP** : PoA to be presented next time.

After being issued with a PoA, the user will be able to use CardSpace in subsequent login attempts from this host machine.

6.5 Discussion

The proposed methods have the potential to increase the security level of ICIM systems, as they mitigate the risk of SPs being deceived by untrustworthy IdPs. They can also help to make the SP's judgement regarding the validity of the security token less critical. This will not only enhance the reliability of the system from the perspective of SPs, but will also indirectly benefit users by reducing the risk to information held by SPs on their behalf. These methods should also reduce the significance of 'token-stealing' attacks, such as those described by Gajek, Schwenk and Xuan [68].

The Proof-of-Authenticity method assumes that the SP supports two authentication mechanisms, one CardSpace-based and the other not (e.g. username/password). This is not an unreasonable assumption, especially as a similar requirement has been discussed in recent CardSpace specifications (see Section 3.3 of [125]).

The proposed challenge-response method is built on the WS-SecurityPolicy standard, which is widely used in ICIM systems. Hence, integrating the method into currently deployed ICIM systems should be straightforward.

Finally, it merits mentioning that a solution similar to the Proof-of-Authenticity method can also be used with Federated identity management systems, and it offers similar advantages for such schemes. However, it would not be a straightforward task to implement a scheme similar to the Challenge-Response method in a Federated identity management system, since there is no SP policy-negotiation step during the authentication process.

6.6   Limitations

One possible disadvantage of the proposed methods is that they have an impact on user mobility. This can be addressed by storing the *PoA* or the user keys on a portable security token such as a smart card, or by storing them at a trusted third party (or TTP). The latter approach would, however, add complexity to the system.

One obvious limitation of the Proof-of-Authenticity method is that it requires the user to be authenticated at least once using another technique before the ICIM system can be used. However, the security risks of this limitation do not appear to be significant, especially if the user is a frequent visitor to the SP's web site.

A limitation of the Challenge-Response method is that it requires modifications to the ICIM-enabling components on the user machine (i.e. the Identity Selector), and the SP server (including the SP *Security Token Service*, an SP server based component responsible for declaring the SP security policy and managing received security tokens).

Another limitation of the Challenge-Response method is that, in the MACed-response mechanism, there is a risk of a malicious IdP masquerading as one of its client users to register with an SP. In such a case, the malicious IdP could obtain the shared secret key from the SP, and thus would be able to produce valid responses to SP challenges. This risk could be mitigated if the SP performs a robust user authentication procedure during the registration process. For example, the SP could ask the registrant to submit an activation-code sent to the submitted email address and/or mobile number, or it could ask the registrant to enter the last three digits printed on the reverse of the credit card for a submitted card number.

A further limitation is the key management overhead. However, if the shared key is compromised or stolen by an attacker, then it would not by itself give immediate access to the SP, since it only provides an additional layer of authentication. That is, the key management process is arguably less security-critical than in many other applications.

6.7 Conclusions

In this chapter we have proposed two independent methods to enhance user authentication in ICIM systems, namely the Proof-of-Authenticity method and the Challenge-Response method. These methods, if implemented correctly, provide the SP with an implicit indication that a log-in attempt was initiated by the legitimate user. A proof-of-concept implementation of the first method has been described.

The proposed techniques add a certain degree of complexity and overhead to the system. However, implementing them should help to enhance the accuracy of the SP judgement of the authenticity of the user.

CHAPTER 7

Integrating Information Card-based and Federated identity management systems

Contents

Over the last few years, many identity management schemes and frameworks have been proposed; however they are typically not interoperable. In this chapter we pro-

pose an approach to enable interoperation between two of the most widely discussed identity management schemes, namely the Liberty Alliance Project ID-WSF LEC SSO profile (a Federated identity management scheme) and the Microsoft CardSpace framework (a ICIM scheme). This approach to integration enhances the practicality of both schemes by enabling users to make use of identity management systems even if other system participants are using different schemes. The main advantages and disadvantages of the proposed integration model are described. A prototype implementation of the proposed integration scheme is also discussed. Much of the material in this chapter has previously been published in [8, 10].

7.1 Introduction

As we have described, a number of identity management systems have been proposed and deployed. These systems are typically not interoperable, which makes it difficult to use them in open environments such as the Internet.

This chapter proposes an approach designed to help address this problem. Specifically, it proposes a method to enable interoperation between the Liberty Alliance Project and the Microsoft CardSpace schemes (see Sections 4.2 and 4.4).

The remainder of this chapter is organised as follows. Section 7.2 presents the proposed integration model, and the message flows are described in Section 7.3. In Section 7.4 we provide an operational analysis, and in Section 7.5 we describe a prototype implementation. Section 7.6 contains a brief review of related work, and Section 7.7 concludes the chapter.

185

7.2 The Integration Model

We first observe that there is a noticeable similarity between the message flow within the ID-WSF LEC SSO profile and the message flow within CardSpace. This similarity can be exploited in order to enable interoperation between the two identity management schemes, which is the approach followed here. This section presents the motivation for this integration proposal, and provides a preliminary discussion of possible integration scenarios.

7.2.1 Motivation

Liberty is currently one of the leading federated identity management systems, and has gained the acceptance of a number of technology-leading companies and organisations. In parallel with this, ICIM systems have emerged during the last few years, and have gained the support of well-known organisations such as Microsoft. Probably the best known ICIM system is CardSpace. CardSpace is deployed freely with Windows Vista and Windows 7, and can also be installed on Windows XP systems. However, CardSpace currently only works on Windows platforms, a situation which seems likely to continue, at least for the near future [20]. Given the wide use of Windows, CardSpace is likely to have a significant impact despite this restriction.

Because of their practical importance, enabling interoperation between Liberty and CardSpace is likely to be of significant benefit to a wide range of service providers and users, and will enhance the practicality of both systems. It seems that interoperation between Liberty and CardSpace can be achieved by integrating their frameworks, and this is the approach we follow here.

As stated in Section 3.3.4.2, a number of other ICIM identity selectors have been developed by a variety of bodies, including the open source community. These schemes can be used on a range of operating systems. One example is provided by DigitalMe[1], which can be regarded as providing CardSpace-like functionality for platforms using the Mac operating system. Given that these rival schemes tend to use a very similar message flow to CardSpace, we believe that the integration approach described in this chapter will also work with such schemes, although the details remain a topic for future research.

We conclude by considering why we have chosen to develop a method of interoperation between CardSpace and Liberty ID-WSF LEC SSO profile as opposed to other Liberty frameworks. The main reason for pursuing this approach is the similarity between the CardSpace framework and Liberty ID-WSF LEC SSO profile; this similarity can be exploited to enable interoperability between Liberty and CardSpace. In particular, both frameworks:

1. require the existence of an enabling component on the user machine;

2. do not require 'identity federation';

3. can be used for both authentication and authorisation;

4. support SAML 2.0 assertions; and

5. require IdP discovery to be performed on the user machine.

7.2.2 Discussion

In the case where all SPs and IdPs support at least one of the two identity management systems (either Liberty or CardSpace, or both), Windows users will face one of the following four scenarios:

---

[1]http://code.bandit-project.org/trac/wiki/DigitalMe

- *Scenario A*: The IdP supports only one identity management system (either Liberty or CardSpace). In this case, users are only able to access SPs using the identity management system supported by their IdP. This appears likely to be the most common case.

- *Scenario B*: The IdP supports both identity management systems (Liberty and CardSpace). In this case, the IdP performs the potentially onerous task of maintaining two different identity management systems, thereby providing flexibility to users when they federate their identities with SPs/RPs. Users are able to access services provided by SPs regardless of which identity management system they adopt.

- *Scenario C*: The SP supports both identity management systems (Liberty and CardSpace). In this case, the SP performs the potentially onerous task of maintaining two different identity management systems. Users are able to access services provided by the SP regardless of which identity management system they adopt.

- *Scenario D*: The User Agent supports both identity management systems (Liberty and CardSpace). In this case, the user agent performs the potentially onerous task of maintaining two different identity management systems. Users are able to access services provided by an SP regardless of which identity management system that it adopts. In this case, the user agent will convert the security tokens (or assertions) to suit the SP. Such an approach relies on the fact that CardSpace can support any token type.

In Scenario A, Windows users have a compatibility problem if the SP is CardSpace-Enabled while their IdP is Liberty-Enabled, or vice versa. Table 7.1 shows the applicability of the identity management systems in the four possible cases, where L-E stands for Liberty Enabled, and CS-E stands for CardSpace Enabled. The ($\checkmark$) sign indicates that there is no compatibility problem, whereas the ($\times$) sign indicates the opposite.

Table 7.1: The applicability of the identity management systems.

User Agent	L-E IdP L-E SP	CS-E IdP CS-E SP	L-E IdP CS-E SP	CS-E IdP L-E SP
Unenhanced	×	×	×	×
L-E	✓	×	×	×
CS-E	×	✓	×	×
L-E and CS-E	✓	✓	×	×

A number of integration models for identity management systems have been proposed (see Section 4.8.1), many of which are based on scenarios B or C (or both). One example is provided by the method of integration proposed by Project Concordia (see Section 4.8.1).

Although most of the integration models are based on scenarios B or C, some SPs and IdPs may not be prepared to accept the burden of supporting two identity management systems and maintaining them simultaneously, at least unless there is a significant financial incentive. Currently, major Internet players such as MSN[2] do not support any integration model for identity management systems. We therefore have reason to believe that an integration model based on scenario D could be practically useful. However, no integration model for web-based identity management based on scenario D has previously been proposed.

The CardSpace identity management system consists of two parts:

1. *The user agent supporting components*: i.e. the Service Requestor and the Identity Selector. These components are responsible for managing the cards and communicating with other parties in the model. It appears that these components could be integrated with Liberty ID-WSF services; however, how this might be achieved remains a possible topic for future research.

---

[2]http://www.msn.com

2. *The Identity Framework*: i.e. the message flow and rules for communication between the parties. This framework is similar to the Liberty ID-WSF LEC SSO profile, in which the user agent is 'Liberty-enabled' in the same way as the user agent is 'CardSpace-enabled' in the CardSpace framework.

In Section 7.3 we propose an integration model enabling interoperation between the Liberty ID-WSF LEC SSO profile and CardSpace, based on scenario D.

7.3 Integrating the Two Schemes

We introduce the notion of an identity management system adaptor that can convert messages between the Liberty-enabling and CardSpace-enabling components. The adaptor resides in the user's machine. It gives the user the ability to use any IdP, and access a service provided by any SP (as long as they are either CardSpace-enabled or Liberty-enabled). This means that, in the presence of such an adaptor, we can change the last two entries in the fifth row of table 7.1 to ($\checkmark$) instead of ($\times$), which implies that such a user would have the ability to make use of an identity system regardless of the identity management system adopted by the SP. That is, this scheme is designed to resolve the incompatibility situation that may occur if the IdP is Liberty-enabled and the RP is CardSpace-enabled, or vice versa.

The *identity management system adaptor* is a piece of software installed on the user's machine which understands both the Liberty and CardSpace frameworks, and their message flows and formats. The adaptor's main job is to interpose itself between the IdPs and the SPs adhering to different identity management systems, in order to translate messages generated by one party to the format understood by the other. The adaptor is triggered when a user agent tries to access an SP that does not support the same identity management system as the IdP that issued the user's

190

identity. We give operational details of the identity management system adaptor later in this section.

7.3.1 Restrictions and assumptions

Before presenting the integration model and its message flow, we note certain restrictions on its operation:

1. In the case of an L-E IdP and a CS-E SP, we assume that the CardSpace-enabled SP does not employ an STS, and as a result it accepts pure SAML tokens [125]. That is the security token supplied to the SP must not be encapsulated within a WS-Trust envelope, as discussed in Section 4.2.1.

2. In the case of an CS-E IdP and an L-E SP, we assume that the IdP generates a pure SAML token.

3. Only asymmetric proof-of-rightful-possession techniques are permitted for the security token. Mapping between the SAML *HoK* and the ICIM *asymmetric* proof-of-rightful-possession methods can be performed using a relatively simple process.

4. For a CardSpace-enabled SP and a Liberty-enabled IdP, the identity management system adaptor will discard any token freshness restrictions requests imposed by the SP, since the Liberty-enabled IdP may not be capable of understanding them.

5. No end-to-end encryption is performed at the application layer; however, the confidentiality of the messages will be preserved using a secure channel (e.g. as provided by SSL/TLS or IPsec).

6. In the case of an L-E IdP and a CS-E SP, we assume that the IdP is prepared to receive the PPID value from the enabling component, and to include it in

the signed SAML assertion within the attribute statement.

7. A CS-E SP must be able to verify an L-E IdP's digital signature within a security token, and vice versa.

As discussed in Sections 4.2 and 4.4, CardSpace is built on a number of WS-* protocols (including WS-SecurityPolicy, WS-MetaDataExchange, and WS-Trust), whereas Liberty does not support these WS-* protocols. The problem this poses to the design of a client-based adaptor is avoided by assuming that a CS-E SP does not employee an STS, and that the IdP generates pure SAML tokens (See the first two assumption above). That is, we assume that the SP does not use the WS-* protocols.

In the case of an L-E IdP and a CS-E SP, the value of the PPID can be included in the token and signed by the IdP using the LibertyCard technique discussed in 7.5. Contrariwise, in the case of an CS-E IdP and a L-E SP, the SP will not expect a specific user pseudonym to be included the SAML assertion, since there is no requirement for 'identity federation' in the LEC profile.

7.3.2 Message flows

Figure 7.1 shows the message flow for the integration model in the case where the IdP is CardSpace-enabled and the SP is Liberty-enabled. This model is based on the frameworks described in Sections 4.2.1 and 4.4.1.1 (the ID-WSF LEC SSO profile is almost identical to the ID-FF LEC profile, except that it supports SAML 2.0 assertions and the IdP is capable of asserting user attributes). Note that the Liberty-Enabling component must be active on the user's PC prior to performing the protocol, and the CardSpace component (i.e. the Identity Selector) must be active on the user machine prior to step 3 of the protocol. The message flow is as follows.

1. **LEUA → SP** : Service Request (HTTP Request with Liberty Enabled Header)

2. **SP → LEUA** : Authentication Request + 'optionally' an IdPs List

   - [The identity management system adaptor replaces the Liberty `Authentication Request`, received from the SP, with a CardSpace `OBJECT tag`, and forwards it to the Identity Selector]

3. **Identity Selector ↔ User** : User picks an InfoCard

4. **Identity Selector → IdP-STS** : RST message

5. **Identity Selector ↔ IdP-STS** : User Authentication

6. **IdP-STS → Identity Selector** : Identity Selector retrieves the requested SAML assertion (RSTR message)

   - [The identity management system adaptor forwards the retrieved SAML assertion to the Liberty-enabling component]

7. **LEUA → SP** : SAML-Assertion (within the HTML Form)

8. **SP → LEUA** : Service Granted!

Figure 7.2 shows the message flow for the integration model in the case where the IdP is Liberty-enabled and the SP is CardSpace-enabled. This model is based on the frameworks described in Sections 4.2.1 and 4.4.1.1. Note that the Liberty-Enabling component must be active on the user's machine prior to step 4 of the protocol, and the CardSpace component (i.e. the Identity Selector) must be active on the user's machine prior to step 3 of the protocol. In this case, the message flow is as follows.

1. **CEUA → SP** : User clicks on the CardSpace logo on the SP log-in web page

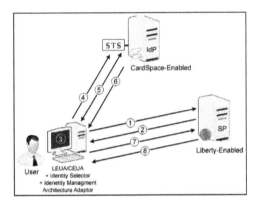

Figure 7.1: Message flow within the integration model (a)

2. **SP → CEUA** : CardSpace `object tags` (within an HTML form)

   - [The identity management system adaptor replaces the CardSpace `OBJECT tag`, received from the SP, with a Liberty `Authentication Request`, and forwards it to the Liberty-Enabling component]

3. **LEUA or User** : Selects the IdP to be used

4. **LEUA → IdP** : Authentication Request

5. **LEUA ↔ IdP** : User Authentication

6. **IdP → LEUA** : Authentication Response + SAML-Assertion

   - [The identity management system adaptor forwards the SAML assertion received from the IdP to the Identity Selector]

7. **Identity Selector → SP-STS** : SAML assertion (within the HTML Form)

8. **SP → CEUA** : Welcome, you are now logged in!

Note that in the case of a L-E IdP and CS-E SP, the Authentication Request message that is sent to the IdP must contain a SAML attribute statement request in which the requested attributes (i.e. claims) are listed. Figures 7.3 and 7.4 show examples of a Liberty Authentication Request message and a CardSpace OBJECT tag, respectively. The greyed out fields in Figure 7.3 are optional fields.

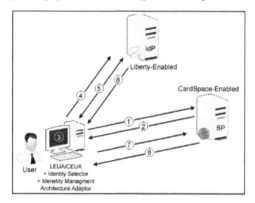

Figure 7.2: Message flow within the integration model (b)

As described above, the identity management system adaptor interposes itself between the IdP and the SP in order to replace and forward messages at certain stages of the protocol run. In summary, the identity management system adaptor software must be capable of performing the following tasks:

- replacing the Liberty Authentication Request, received from the SP, with a CardSpace OBJECT tag, and vice versa;
- forwarding messages and SAML assertions to either Liberty-enabling or CardSpace software components.

Whilst the first task is relatively straightforward, the second is not so simple, since it requires a well-defined set of APIs in order for the identity management system adaptor software to communicate with the Liberty-Enabling and CardSpace components. Fortunately, Microsoft has recently published a set of APIs that enables developers to interact with the CardSpace-enabling components[3]. The precise de-

---

[3]http://msdn.microsoft.com/en-us/library/aa702727.aspx

tails of the operation of the adaptor will therefore depend on how these components are implemented. With regard to Liberty, whereas some enabling products are open, such as the Entr'ouvert Lasso[4], or provide a set of integration APIs, as is the case for HP Select Federation[5], other products, such as CA SiteMinder[6], lack such openness. Indeed, it is possible that the adaptor could be integrated into the Liberty-enabling and CardSpace components.

```
<lib:AuthnRequest
id="12345" RequestID="RPCUk2Il+GVz+t1lLURp51oFvJXk" MajorVersion="1"
MinorVersion="0" IssueInstant="2010-04-19T21:32:5Z"
xmlns:lib="http://projectliberty.org/schemas/core/2002/12">
  <lib:ProviderID>http://ServiceProvider.com</lib:ProviderID>
  <ds:Signature> ... </ds:Signature>
  <lib:ForceAuthn>false</lib:ForceAuthn>
  <lib:IsPassive>false</lib:IsPassive>
  <lib:Federate>false</Federate>
  <lib:ProtocolProfile>http://projectliberty.org/profiles/brws-post
  </lib:ProtocolProfile>
  <lib:AuthnContext>
  <lib:AuthnContextClassRef>
   http://projectliberty.org/schemas/authctx/classes/Password-ProtectedTransport
  </lib:AuthnContextClassRef>
  </lib:AuthnContext>
  <lib:RelayState>
   R0lGODlhcgGSALMAAAOCAEMmCZtuMFQxDS8b
  </lib:RelayState>
  <lib:AuthnContextComparisonType>exact</lib:AuthnContextComparisonType>
</lib:AuthnRequest>
```

Figure 7.3: Liberty Authentication Request message

```
<object type="application/x-informationcard" name="xmlToken">
  <param name="tokenType"
  value="urn:oasis:names:tc:SAML:2.0:assertion" />
  <param name="requiredClaims"
  value="http://schemas.xmlsoap.org/ws/2005/05/identity
  /claims/privatepersonalidentifier" />
  </object>
```

Figure 7.4: CardSpace OBJECT tags

[4]http://lasso.entrouvert.org
[5]http://support.openview.hp.com/encore/ovsf65.jsp
[6]http://www.ca.com/products/product.aspx?id=5262

7.4 An Analysis of the Integration Model

The integration model takes advantage of the similarity between the ID-WSF LEC SSO profile and the CardSpace framework, and this helps to reduce the effort required for full system integration. Moreover, the proposed integration model is designed to be implemented without the need for technical cooperation between Microsoft and Liberty.

Full implementation of the proposed model might be non-trivial, but the benefits could be significant. Lack of interoperability between leading identity management systems could be a major obstacle to the global adoption of such schemes.

It appears that the 'SAML 2.0 InfoCard token profile' described in [38] can be used to build a integration scheme similar to that proposed in this chapter, in particular since it defines InfoCard OBJECT tags that can be processed by the IdP to generate the requested SAML 2.0 assertion. However, the profile specifications are currently only drafts, and a number of detailed issues need to be resolved.

One potential limitation of the proposed model is that the user agent must be both CardSpace-enabled and Liberty-enabled. However, Windows Vista user agents (i.e. browsers) will, by default, be CardSpace-enabled, and to make a browser Liberty-enabled simply requires the installation of certain Java scripts; as a result this does not seem to be a major issue. Another possible limitation of the proposed model is the added restrictions on the token type, encryption and freshness requests; these restrictions will prevent the users from utilising certain features offered by CardSpace. However, these restrictions only affect the CardSpace framework because, from the Liberty perspective, token handling will remain the same [170].

A further possible limitation is the necessity for interactions between the adaptor and the CardSpace-enabling components; because of the closed nature of CardSpace this might not be straightforward. Finally, use of the proposed integration model will result in a delay at the user system while the identity management system adaptor performs the necessary conversions; however, any such delay is likely to be very small.

A similar integration scheme to that proposed here could be used to help develop a scheme that operates with STS-enhanced SPs. The main problem in supporting interoperation with STS-enhanced SPs is that the CardSpace specifications require security tokens (e.g. SAML assertions) to be transferred using specific WS-Trust syntax, to enable information about the token format to be provided. This is because CardSpace can accept any token type, and hence the type of the token must be indicated to the recipient. Thus a CardSpace-enabled SP with an STS would expect received SAML assertions to be encapsulated within a WS-Trust envelope.

In addition, if a CardSpace-enabled SP expects the entire WS-Trust envelope to be signed, then the adaptor cannot create such an envelope from the Liberty IdP provided SAML assertion, since it cannot create the necessary signature. Similarly, if a CardSpace-enabled IdP provides a signed WS-Trust envelope, then an integration adaptor will not be able to use it to obtain a signed assertion suitable for a Liberty-enabled SP. However, as specified in [134, 162], an IdP can choose which fields of the WS-Trust envelope it signs, i.e. it is not obliged to sign the entire envelope. If a CardSpace-enabled IdP only signs the SAML assertion part of the WS-Trust envelope, then an integration adaptor should be able to extract the signed assertion and sent it to a Liberty-enabled SP; similarly, in the case of a Liberty-enabled IdP, an integration adaptor could use the signed SAML assertion provided by the IdP to construct a WS-Trust envelope with the property that only the SAML assertion is signed.

The practicality of this rather more complex scheme cannot be judged without building a prototype implementation. In particular, parsing and converting the XML envelopes is not a straightforward task, and will require further investigation. Investigating this possibility further would make a potentially interesting topic for future research.

7.5 Prototype Implementation

To demonstrate the applicability of the proposed integration model we have implemented a prototype based on the second integration case described in Section 7.3 (i.e. integrating a CS-E SP and an L-E IdP). Using the prototype adaptor, CardSpace users are able to obtain a SAML 2.0 assertions from an L-E IdP that will satisfy the security requirements of a CS-E SP.

In the prototype, the user is not required to install a Liberty-enabling component; the only special requirement is the installation of an 'identity management architecture adaptor' on the user machine. This adaptor has been implemented as a browser extension (or plug-in).

The implemented adaptor plug-in is able to:

- automatically execute;

- read and inspect browser-rendered web pages;

- modify rendered web pages if certain conditions hold;

- intercept, inspect and modify messages exchanged between a CardSpace Identity Selector and a CS-E SP (via a browser);

- automatically forward security tokens (via browser based HTTP redirects) to

199

L-E IdPs and to CS-E SPs; and

- provide a means for the user to enable or disable it.

Since we have assumed that the CS-E SP is not STS-enhanced (see Section 4.2.1), it will express its security policy using HTML/XHTML, and the interactions between the CardSpace Identity Selector and the SP must be based on HTTP(S). This significantly simplifies the job of implementing the adaptor plug-in on the user machine.

We used a simple and efficient method for IdP discovery during execution of the scheme. Either prior to, or during, use of the scheme, the user must create a special self-issued InfoCard (see Section 4.2.1), referred to as a *LibertyCard*, which represents an L-E IdP. This InfoCard must contain the URI of the relevant L-E IdP, and must also contain a predefined sequence of characters, e.g. the word 'Liberty', so that it can be identified. The concept of LibertyCards is discussed in more detail in Section 7.5.3. In the prototype we assume that the CS-E SP gets an assertion from a L-E IdP as a result of a user choosing a LibertyCard via the Identity Selector.

Whenever a self-issued InfoCard is selected by the user, the adaptor plug-in will intercept the internal Identity Selector communications before the SAML 1.1 assertion generated by the SIP is delivered to the CS-E SP. The adaptor plug-in then processes this assertion, and if the value of one of the asserted claims is the word 'Liberty', then this means that the selected InfoCard is a LibertyCard. In this case the adaptor continues; otherwise the adaptor terminates and processing continues as if the adaptor were not present.

7.5.1 The Prototype Framework

As stated above, the prototype implements the second integration case described in Section 7.3. Figure 7.5 provides a sketch of the prototype message flows. The prototype executes the following series of steps.

1. The user employs the CardSpace-enabled User Agent (CEUA), i.e. the browser, to request the CS-E SP log-in web page.

2. The CS-E SP replies with the log-in web page.

3. The adaptor plug-in scans the login page to detect whether or not the SP web site supports CardSpace. If so, it embeds a function into the page to intercept the SAML assertion that will later be returned by the Identity Selector. If not, the adaptor plug-in terminates.

4. The user clicks on the CardSpace logo to log-in.

5. The CS-E SP sends the CardSpace OBJECT tags to trigger the Identity Selector on the user machine. These tags contain the CS-E SP policy.

6. The Identity Selector discovers that there are self-issued InfoCards that can be used with this SP. It displays all such InfoCards to the user.

7. The user selects one of the displayed InfoCards.

8. The Identity Selector sends an RST message to the SIP (see Section 4.2.1) that includes a SAML 1.1 assertion request.

9. The SIP replies with an RSTR message (see Section 4.2.1) that includes a SAML 1.1 assertion, as requested.

10. Unlike during normal CardSpace operation, the RSTR is not sent to the CS-E SP; instead, the adaptor plug-in intercepts the RSTR containing the SAML assertion. If the InfoCard that was selected by the user is a *LibertyCard*, the the adaptor converts the intercepted assertion into a SAML 2.0 assertion

request, embeds it in an Authentication Request message, and forwards it to the appropriate L-E IdP.

11. If necessary, the L-E IdP authenticates the user.

12. The L-E IdP replies with a SAML 2.0 assertion embedded within an Authentication Response message.

13. The adaptor plug-in forwards the assertion to the CS-E SP, optionally after first obtaining permission from the user.

14. The CS-E SP checks the received SAML 2.0 assertion and, if it is valid, the user will be successfully logged-in.

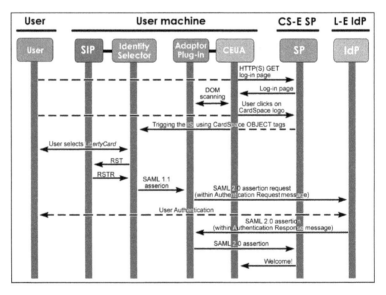

Figure 7.5: Prototype message flows

7.5.2 Technical Details

The prototype is coded as a client-side browser plug-in using JavaScript [145, 149], which was chosen to maximise portability. The implementation uses the Document Object Model (DOM) [81] to inspect and manipulate HTML pages and XML documents. A client-side scripting language can use the DOM to read and modify the contents of a web page or completely alter its appearance. The prototype does not use any of the published CardSpace APIs. This was a deliberate design decision made to ease migration of the plug-in to other ICIM systems.

The adaptor plug-in was built using IE7PRO, an Internet Explorer extension, chosen to simplify implementation of the prototype. Users of the prototype must therefore install IE7PRO, freely available at the IE7PRO web site[7], prior to installing the adaptor plug-in. To enable or disable the integration prototype, a user can simply tick or un-tick the appropriate entry in the 'IE7PRO Preferences' interface. Finally, note that the adaptor plug-in does not require any changes to default Internet Explorer security settings, thereby avoiding potential vulnerabilities resulting from lowered browser security settings.

7.5.3 Operational Details

In this section we describe in detail the operation of the prototype.

Prior to use of the scheme, a *LibertyCard* must be created by the user for the relevant L-E IdP. This involves invoking the Identity Selector on the user machine and inserting the URI of this IdP in the *web page* field[8] and the trigger word 'Liberty' in the *city* field. The user must enter the values of the claims that can be asserted

---

[7]http://www.ie7pro.com

[8]The *web page* field was chosen to contain the Liberty IdP URL since it seemed the logical choice; however, this is an implementation option.

by the L-E IdP; however these values are not required to be correct. For ease of identification, the user can give the personal card a meaningful name, e.g. the organisational name of the IdP. The user can also upload an image for the card, e.g. containing the logo of the IdP. When a user wishes to use a particular L-E IdP, the user simply chooses the corresponding LibertyCard. Below, we give further details of the operation of the adaptor plug-in.

1. In step 3 of the scenario described in Section 7.5.1, and before the HTML login page is displayed, the adaptor plug-in uses the DOM to perform the following sequence of steps.

   (a) The adaptor plug-in scans the web page in the following way:

       i. It searches through the HTML elements of the web page to detect whether any HTML forms are present. If so, it searches each form, scanning through each of its child elements for an HTML OBJECT tag.

       ii. If an OBJECT tag is found, it retrieves and examines its type. If it is of type 'application/xinformationCard' (which signals web site support for CardSpace), it continues; otherwise it aborts.

       iii. It searches through the param tags (child elements of the retrieved CardSpace object tag) for the 'requiredClaims' tag, which lists the claims required by the CS-E SP security policy.

       iv. If the required claims include 'city' attribute, and a self-issued token can be used, then the adaptor will intercept the generated SAML 1.1 assertion.

   (b) The plug-in adds a JavaScript function to the head section of the HTML page to intercept the SAML 1.1 assertion before it is sent back to the CS-E SP by the Identity Selector (in step 9).

   (c) The plug-in obtains the current action attribute of the CardSpace HTML form, encrypts it using AES (see Section 2.3.1.1) with a secret key known only to the adaptor plug-in, and then stores it in the user machine as a cookie. This attribute specifies the endpoint URI at the CS-E SP to which the authentication token must be forwarded for processing. If the obtained attribute is not a fully qualified domain name address, the JavaScript inherent properties, i.e. *document.location.protocol* and *document.location.host*, are used to help reconstruct the full address.

(d) After storing it, the adaptor plug-in changes the current action attribute of the CardSpace HTML form to point to the newly created 'interception' function (see step 2 above).

(e) The adaptor plug-in creates and appends an 'invisible' HTML form to the HTML page to be used later for sending the SAML token request to the L-E IdP.

2. In step 10 of the scenario described in Section 7.5.1, the adaptor plug-in uses the DOM to perform the following sequence of steps.

(a) The function added to the HTML page in step 2 of the previous sequence of steps intercepts the RSTR message sent by the Identity Selector.

(b) It parses the intercepted token. If the *city* field contains the word 'Liberty', the plug-in proceeds; if not, normal operation of CardSpace continues. It also reads the *web page* field to discover the address of the IdP. In addition, all other fields, including the PPID and InfoCard public key with its digital signature, are parsed. The *city, web page*, PPID, and any other supported claims fields will be contained in a SAML attribute statement. The adaptor plug-in uses an XML parser built into the browser to read and manipulate the intercepted XML token. The adaptor plug-in passes the token to the parser, which reads it and converts it into an XML DOM object that can be accessed and manipulated by JavaScript. The DOM views the XML token as a tree-structure, thereby enabling

JavaScript to traverse the DOM tree to read (and possibly modify) the content of the token elements. New elements can also be created where necessary.

(c) It converts the token format from a SAML 1.1 response message into a SAML 2.0 request message. The adaptor plug-in also adds the PPID and the InfoCard public key along with its signature to the SAML request message, because the token must be signed by the L-E IdP to provide integrity and authenticity services.

(d) It writes the entire SAML request message as a hidden variable into the invisible HTML form created earlier.

(e) It retrieves the encrypted CS-E SP endpoint URI from the cookie, and writes it into the invisible form as a hidden variable.

(f) It writes the URL address of the L-E IdP into the action attribute of the invisible form.

(g) It auto-submits the HTML form (transparently to the user), using the JavaScript method 'click()' on the 'submit' tag.

To implement steps 10 to 12 of the scenario described in Section 7.5.1, we created an experimental web site to act as an L-E IdP. PHP is used to enable the IdP to parse the SAML request and perform the user authentication. The user credentials, i.e. username and password, that the IdP uses to authenticate the user are stored in a MySQL database. They are salted, hashed with SHA-1 (see Section 2.3.3), and protected against SQL injection attacks. The prototype uses an XML DOM parser.

3. In step 13 of the scenario described in Section 7.5.1, the adaptor plug-in performs the following sequence of steps.

(a) It obtains the encrypted value of the CS-E SP endpoint URI from the appropriate HTML hidden variable, decrypts it using its internally stored secret key, and inserts it into the action attribute of the HTML form carrying the received SAML 2.0 assertion.

(b) The adaptor plug-in then displays the token to the user and requests consent to proceed. The displayed token indicates the types of information the authentication token is carrying, as well as the exact CS-E SP endpoint address to which the token will be forwarded. The JavaScript 'confirm()' pop-up box is used to achieve this.

(c) If the user has given approval, the plug-in seamlessly submits the security token (i.e. the SAML 1.1 assertion) to the CS-E SP using the JavaScript 'click()' method.

To test the prototype, we built an experimental web site to act as a CS-E SP. On receipt of the SAML authentication token, the SP uses PHP in step 14 to parse and validate the received token. As is the case with the Liberty IdP, the user identifying data is salted, hashed and stored in a MySQL database that is resistant to SQL injection attacks. The validation process includes verifying the digital signatures and checking the conditions, such as the time stamps, included in the token. The PPID and the InfoCard public key in the token are compared to the values stored in the CS-E SP database, and the authentication status is also checked.

7.6   Related Work

Unlike the integration model proposed in this chapter, the Project Concordia integration framework described in Section 4.8.1 is mainly based on scenarios B and C (as described in Section 7.2.2); however, it could also be used as the basis for building a Liberty/CardSpace integration model by taking advantage of the similarities between the Liberty ID-FF SSO profiles and the SAML SSO profiles.

The integration model proposed by Jorstada et al. [110] (as described in Section 2.8.1) is also quite different to the model we have proposed in this chapter.

SWITCH[9] is developing specifications for an interoperability framework that would support the exchange of WS-Trust messages in the Liberty ID-WSF [107]. Such specifications might be useful for building a CardSpace/Liberty ID-WSF integration model, and for mapping the necessary security tokens.

Finally, since the work described in this chapter was completed, it has become apparent that Liberty is also working on a somewhat similar solution. No specifications have yet been released, but the plans are apparent from a presentation available at the Liberty web site[10].

7.7   Conclusions

In this chapter we have proposed an integration model enabling interoperation between Liberty and CardSpace. This integration model takes advantage of the similarities between the Liberty ID-FF LEC framework and the CardSpace message flows. The proposed integration model is based on a client-side identity management system adaptor that converts the format of messages within the message flows of the two schemes. We have also presented an analysis of the main limitations and benefits of the integration model, and described a prototype implementation.

The model is designed to integrate two frameworks with somewhat different scopes, and this has caused certain technical problems which have been described and analysed. We have also proposed possible solutions for such problems.

---

[9]http://www.switch.ch

[10]http://projectliberty.org/liberty/content/download/4541/31033/file/20080911-ICP-Cardspace-DIDW.pdf

7.7 Conclusions

Enabling interoperation between two of the most widely discussed identity management systems should help to enhance the practicality and the usability of both CardSpace and Liberty. This could be of major benefit to both the users and implementers of these systems.

CHAPTER 8

A delegation framework for Federated identity management systems

Contents

Building support for delegation services into a Federated identity management system enhances its flexibility and scalability. Users may need to delegate all (or a subset) of their access rights or privileges to other parties in the system. However, some Federated identity management systems lack such support. For example, the Liberty Alliance project does not include delegation functionality in its specifications.

In this chapter we propose a delegation framework for Liberty that can be readily integrated into the current specifications. The delegation scheme takes advantage of the trust relationships that exist by definition within the Liberty circles of trust, and is based on extending the use of attribute statements in SAML assertions. The framework is built on the Liberty ID-WSF SAML 2.0 SSO profiles, and supports both direct and indirect delegation. Finally, the approach proposed in this chapter can be applied to any Federated identity management system built on the SAML SSO profiles. Much of the material in this chapter has previously been published in [11].

8.1   Introduction

As discussed in Chapter 3, federated identity management systems are based on the notion of sharing authentication information between an IdP and SPs within a certain CoT. The access rights given to a particular user by an SP are determined in accordance with the shared authentication information. Providing support for delegation services (see Section 2.2.3) in a Federated identity management system should help to enhance its practicality by improving its flexibility and scalability.

Support for delegation needs to build upon the trust relationship between the IdP and the SP. Helpfully, most Federated identity management systems provide reliable approaches for transforming sensitive information about the system users (e.g. using SAML, SOAP and WS-*), and these approaches can be used to help support delegation.

Whilst some Federated identity management systems, such as Shibboleth, support delegation services (see Section 4.8.2.1), the current Liberty specifications lack such a provision[1]. However, the Liberty ID-WSF frameworks (see Section 4.4) provide

---

[1]As discussed in Section 4.4.1.2, the ID-WSF People Service does support sharing of access to information, but this falls short of full delegation functionality.

a solid basis on which to build customised delegation services. In this chapter we extend the use of SAML to support delegation services.

The remainder of this chapter is organised as follows. In Section 8.2 we discuss the advantages of supporting delegation services within the Liberty framework. Section 8.3 proposes a delegation framework for Liberty, and Section 8.4 proposes additional services and enhancements. Section 8.5 discusses related issues, and Section 8.6 concludes the chapter.

8.2 Delegation and Liberty

Although Liberty does not specify a delegation model, supporting delegation would potentially enhance systems adopting the Liberty specifications. In this chapter we adhere to the conceptual delegation model described in Section 2.2.3.

As an example, we consider the hypothetical Liberty framework shown in figure 8.1, in which there are two SPs, an estate agent and a bank, and a single IdP that has a federation agreement with both SPs. Suppose that a user who has accounts with both SPs and with the IdP (and whose SP accounts are federated with her/his IdP account), wants to make an offer to purchase a house advertised by the estate agent (SP1) web site. In order to approve the proposed purchase, the estate agent must check the financial status of the user to determine whether or not she/he can afford to buy the selected house. Since the web site of the bank that holds the user's account is in a CoT that includes the estate agent web site, both SPs (i.e. the estate agent and the bank) trust the same IdP.

The Liberty *Discovery Service* (or DS) described in Section 4.4.1.2 can be used to enable the user to delegate to the estate agent the ability to get information about

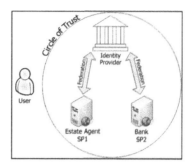

Figure 8.1: Liberty model

her/his financial status from the bank. However, what if, for example, the bank needs to access a third SP to obtain the requested information? The DS does not support services such as re-delegation, delegation-revocation, and role-delegation. To support such services, a full delegation system would need to be built in which the IdP plays the role of a delegation authority and issues delegation assertions (see Section 2.2.3).

The infrastructure to build a delegation framework for Liberty is already in place; for example, Liberty supports a number of data transport and security protocols such as SAML, SOAP and WS-Security. These techniques can be used to transport sensitive information for delegation purposes (notably delegation assertions). Moreover, Liberty DS can be used to address many related issues such as, for example, mapping user pseudonyms.

8.3   A Delegation Framework for Liberty

In this section we describe the form of the delegation assertion used in the proposed delegation framework. We also propose a delegation framework for Liberty.

8.3.1 The Delegation Assertion

Before we present the delegation scheme, we describe the structure of the delegation assertion on which it is based. As stated above, the scheme extends the attribute statement in the SAML assertion (see section 2.4.2) to build a delegation assertion. Although we use SAML 2.0 to build the delegation assertion, it is also possible to use SAML 1.* to build a similar assertion, although this would require some minor changes to the assertion syntax.

The delegation assertion is issued and signed by the IdP, and should not be issued without explicit consent from the user (or the privilege owner). This consent can be given *online*, by asking the user directly at the time of delegation, or can be given in advance or *offline* (e.g. by telling the IdP in advance that any delegation request made at a particular time with particular delegatees should always be approved). The IdP's signature on the assertion implicitly indicates user consent.

As discussed in Section 3.3.4.3, the IdP will have established pseudonyms for a user with an SP if that user has federated its SP-issued identity to its IdP-issued identity. The delegation scheme requires the *delegator* (i.e. the user) to have federated its identity, issued by the *delegation assertion target* (i.e. the SP that holds the resource to which access is to be delegated), to its IdP-issued identity. Hence the IdP that is acting as a *delegation authority* shares pseudonyms for the user with the delegation assertion target. To provide a degree of anonymity, the ID of the user included within the assertion is a pseudonym that is only understood by the delegation assertion target (i.e. all other SPs within the CoT learn nothing from observing the pseudonym). The pseudonym is encrypted using the delegation assertion target's public key. This approach enables the delegator to be identified by the target SP in a way that preserves user privacy. Please note that Liberty DS handles user pseudonyms using a very similar approach (see Section 4.4.1.2).

The delegatee can demonstrate its rightful possession of the delegation assertion using the HoK proof-of-rightful-possession (or subject confirmation) method offered by SAML (see Section 3.3.4.3).

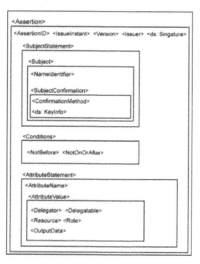

Figure 8.2: Structure of the delegation assertion

Figure 8.2 shows the structure of the delegation assertion. The `<AttributeStatement>` is extended to include new tags for delegation purposes. A delegation assertion contains the following fields.

- `<Issuer>` : The URI of the IdP that issued the assertion.

- `<ds: Signature>` : The IdP's signature on the entire assertion.

- `<Subject>` : The URI of the delegatee, the confirmation method to be used (which here must be HoK) and the confirmation data. It also contains information about the delegatee's public key that is to be used to verify the confirmation data.

- `<Conditions>` : Constraints that apply to the delegation (e.g. the validity

215

duration of the assertion, and/or the URI of the entity to receive the assertion). In SAML 2.0, this item can be extended to include any required conditions.

- `<AttributeStatement>` : Information about the delegation act, in the form of assertion attributes. The defined attributes are:

  - `<Delegator>` : The pseudonym of the user (or the privilege owner) that is agreed by the IdP and the target SP. This attribute is encrypted using the target SP's public key.

  - `<Delegatable>` : A boolean value that indicates whether or not the assertion is delegatable (i.e. whether or not indirect delegation is allowed).

  - `<Resource>` : The URI of the target SP resource.

  - `<Role>` : If the user has multiple access control roles at the target SP system, she/he can also use this attribute to specify which role is to be delegated to the delegatee.

  - `<OutputData>` : A boolean value that indicates whether or not the result data should be encrypted using the delegatee's public key.

The *Role* field must be encoded in an agreed way so that the delegation assertion target (i.e. the target SP) can understand and act upon it [46, 49]. We assume here that the target SP is capable of understanding the syntax and semantics of the delegated roles. All the existing SAML-based delegation schemes of which the author is aware (such as those given in [72, 176]) make the same assumption.

Figure 8.5 provides an example of a delegation assertion. Figure 8.4 gives an *XML Schema* for the proposed tags; an equivalent *DTD* is as shown in Figure 8.3.

```
<!ELEMENT AttributeStatement (Delegator, Delegatable, Resource,
Role, OutputData)>
<!ELEMENT Delegator (#PCDATA)>
<!ELEMENT Delegatable EMPTY>
<!ATTLIST Delegatable Indirect (True | False) "False">
<!ELEMENT Resource (#PCDATA)>
<!ELEMENT Role (#PCDATA)>
<!ELEMENT OutputData EMPTY>
<!ATTLIST OutputData Encrypted (True | False) "False">
```

Figure 8.3: A DTD for the proposed tags

8.3.2 Delegation Protocols

The delegation framework is based on the ID-WSF SAML 2.0 SSO profiles. The three relevant profiles are the *artifact* profile, the *POST* profile and the *enabled-client* profile. In this section we describe three variants of the Liberty delegation scheme modelled on these three profiles. We emphasise here that in every case all the message transfers in must be carried over a secure channel, e.g. as provided by SSL/TLS (see Section 2.4.1), IPsec [115] or SSH [183].

8.3.2.1 Delegation Framework Based on the Artifact Profile

The message flow is summarised in figure 8.6, and it is as follows.

1. The user requests a service from SP1 using the user agent.

2. SP1 decides that the required service cannot be provided without first obtaining certain data from SP2. SP1 redirects the user agent to the IdP's web site, along with a delegation assertion request embedded within an HTML GET or POST command. This request should include information about the delegatee (i.e. SP1), the target SP (i.e. SP2) and the confirmation data to be included in the token.

217

```
<xs:schema xmlns:xs="http://www.w3.org/2001/XMLSchema" elementFormDefault="qualified">
 <xs:import namespace="http://www.w3.org/XML/1998/namespace"/>
  <xs:element name="AttributeStatement">
   <xs:complexType>
    <xs:sequence>
      <xs:element ref="Delegator"/>
      <xs:element ref="Delegatable"/>
      <xs:element ref="Resource"/>
      <xs:element ref="Role"/>
      <xs:element ref="OutputData"/>
    </xs:sequence>
   </xs:complexType>
  </xs:element>
   <xs:element name="Delegator" type="xs:string"/>
   <xs:element name="Delegatable">
    <xs:complexType>
     <xs:sequence>
      <xs:any minOccurs="0" maxOccurs="unbounded" namespace="##any" processContents="lax">
       <xs:annotation>
        <xs:documentation>
          Any xml content is allowed in this element.
        </xs:documentation>
       </xs:annotation>
      </xs:any>
     </xs:sequence>
     <xs:attribute name="Indirect" type="xs:boolean" default="false" />
    </xs:complexType>
   </xs:element>
   <xs:element name="Resource" type="xs:string"/>
   <xs:element name="Role" type="xs:string"/>
   <xs:element name="OutputData">
    <xs:complexType>
     <xs:sequence>
      <xs:any minOccurs="0" maxOccurs="unbounded" namespace="##any" processContents="lax">
       <xs:annotation>
        <xs:documentation>
          Any xml content is allowed in this element.
        </xs:documentation>
       </xs:annotation>
      </xs:any>
     </xs:sequence>
     <xs:attribute name="Encrypted" type="xs:boolean" default="false" \>
    </xs:complexType>
   </xs:element>
</xs:schema>
```

Figure 8.4: XML schema for the delegation tags

3. After receiving the delegation assertion request, the IdP checks whether it has a federation relationship for this user with the target SP. If so, then the IdP checks whether the user has already provided consent to such a delegation (i.e. offline consent). If not, then the IdP must, by some means (e.g. an interactive dialogue box), ask the user for consent to the delegation (i.e. to grant SP1 permission to obtain the required information from SP2 on her/his behalf) and whether or not the user wishes the result to be encrypted. Once user consent has been obtained, the IdP creates a delegation assertion and gives it a 'reference' string (known as a SAML artifact). Subsequently, the IdP directs

218

```
<Assertion ID="1234abcd" IssueInstant="2007-07-01T00:22:02Z" Version="2.0">
<Issuer> .. The URI of the IdP .. </Issuer>
<ds:Signature> .. The IdP's Singature .. </ds:Signature>

<Subject>
<NameID> .. The URI of the Delegatee .. </NameID>
<SubjectConfirmation Method="urn:oasis:names:tc:SAML:2.0:cm:holder-of-key">
<ds:KeyInfo> .. The Delegatee's key information .. </ds:KeyInfo>
.. Confirmation Data ..
</SubjectConfirmationData>
</SubjectConfirmation>
</Subject>

<Conditions NotBefore="2007-07-05T08:20:05Z"
NotOnOrAfter="2007-07-05T08:24:05Z">
<AudienceRestriction>
<Audience> .. The URI of the assertion receiver .. </Audience>
</AudienceRestriction>
</Conditions>

<AttributeStatement>
<Delegator>
.. Encrypted pseudonym of the user ..
</Delegator>
<Delegatable Indirect="false">
.. Related data can be placed here ..
</Delegatable>
<Resource>
.. The URI where the requested resource is located ..
</Resource>
<Role>
.. The delegated role ..
</Role>
<OutputData Encrypted="false">
.. Related data can be placed here ..
</OutputData>
</AttributeStatement>

</Assertion>
```

Figure 8.5: Example of delegation assertion

the user agent to SP1's web site, along with the assertion reference embedded within an HTML GET or POST command.

4. SP1 sends a SAML assertion request that includes the reference received in step 3 to the IdP.

5. The IdP sends the delegation assertion to SP1 in which the user is the delegator and SP1 is the subject.

6. SP1 forwards the delegation assertion to the target SP (i.e. SP2). Steps 4, 5 and 6 are conveyed over SOAP. If the delegation is approved by SP2, and the

delegator (i.e. the user) is authorised to access the requested data (or perform the requested task), then SP2 proceeds with the requested action.

7. SP2 sends the resulting data to SP1 (SP2 will first encrypt the resulting data using SP1's public key, if requested to do so in the delegation assertion).

8. SP1 grants the user the requested service (or sends the requested data to the user).

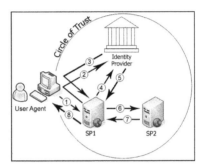

Figure 8.6: Delegation framework based on the artifact profile

8.3.2.2 Delegation Framework Based on the POST Profile

The message flow is summarised in figure 8.7. In the POST profile there is no direct communication between the delegatee (i.e. SP1) and the delegation authority (i.e. the IdP).

The first two steps of this profile are identical to the first two steps of the artifact profile. However, in step 3, instead of sending an assertion reference to SP1 (via the user agent), the IdP itself sends the delegation assertion to SP1, after embedding it within an HTML form and redirecting the user agent to SP1's URI. Steps 4, 5 and 6 are identical to steps 6, 7 and 8 of the artifact profile.

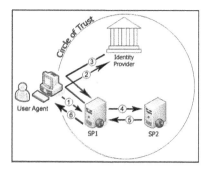

Figure 8.7: Delegation framework based on the POST profile

8.3.2.3 Delegation Framework Based on the enabled-client Profile

The message flow is summarised in figure 8.8. This profile requires the user agent
to be Liberty-enabled (i.e. to be capable of understanding and processing SAML
assertion requests and responses); this can be achieved by installing appropriate
software components on the user machine.

The first step is similar to the first step of the artifact and POST profiles. In step
2, SP1 sends a delegation assertion request (including the confirmation data) to the
user agent, and in step 3 the user agent forwards the assertion request to the IdP.
In step 4, the IdP sends the delegation assertion to the user agent, after approving
the request and obtaining user consent. Steps 3 and 4 are conveyed over SOAP. In
step 5, the user forwards the delegation assertion to SP1 by embedding it within an
HTML form. Steps 6, 7 and 8 of this profile are identical to steps 6, 7 and 8 of the
artifact profile described in section 8.3.2.1.

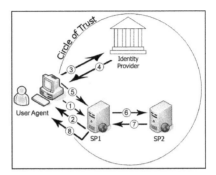

Figure 8.8: Delegation framework based on the enabled-client profile

8.4 Additional Services

In this section we discuss a number of possible enhancements to the proposed delegation framework.

8.4.1 Indirect Delegation

Although the delegation scheme described in section 8.3.2 supports direct delegation, the framework can be extended to also support indirect delegation (see Section 2.2.3).

Before we describe the proposed indirect delegation scheme, we first list certain prerequisites for its operation. We assume that:

- the user has informed the IdP in advance (i.e. offline) of all the SPs that can participate in any indirect delegation sequence along with the privileges that can be delegated to each SP;

- the user has already delegated an SP, SP1 say, to obtain specific data from another SP, SP2 say, using one of the delegation protocols described in 8.3.2;

and

- when the user gave consent for the delegation to SP1 of the right to access certain services provided by SP2, the user also agreed (e.g. via a dialogue box) to permit indirect delegation in the current working session. This consent is indicated by setting the value of the *indirect* attribute in the `<Delegatable>` element to 'true'.

The message flow of the indirect delegation scheme is sketched in Figure 8.9, and operates as follows.

1. After receiving the delegation assertion from SP1, we suppose that SP2 cannot deliver the requested service (or data) without first obtaining certain user-related data from another SP, SP3 say. Accordingly, SP2 requests a new (or revised) delegation assertion from the IdP to allow it to act as a delegatee in requesting service from the new target, SP3. As part of the request it forwards the delegation assertion it received from SP1.

2. The IdP checks SP2's request to act as a delegatee and the forwarded delegation assertion. It first checks whether or not the delegation is delegatable (i.e. it checks the *indirect* attribute of the `<Delegatable>` element). It also checks whether the user has consented to delegation to the new delegatee (in the case of indirect delegation, user consent must be obtained in advance). If (and only if) all the checks succeed, the IdP issues SP2 with a revised delegation assertion that can be used to obtain the requested data or service from SP3. Note that the subject of the newly issued delegation assertion must be the new delegatee (i.e. SP2). The URI of SP2 along with information about its public key must be included in the `<Subject>` element. Moreover, the `<Delegator>` element must contain the pseudonym of the user that is used in communications between the IdP and SP3, and must be encrypted using SP3's public key

(i.e. the user remains the delegator in all delegation steps).

3. SP2 forwards the 'revised' delegation assertion to SP3.

4. SP3 checks the validity of the received delegation assertion. If the assertion is valid and the delegated privileges are sufficient to obtain the requested data, then SP3 sends the requested data to SP2.

5. SP2 delivers the requested service (or data) to SP1.

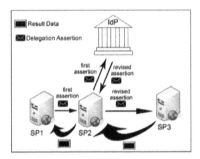

Figure 8.9: Indirect delegation scheme

As shown in Figure 8.10, the above process can be applied iteratively if further transfers of delegation are required. The IdP can, optionally, provide the user with a list of all the participating SPs.

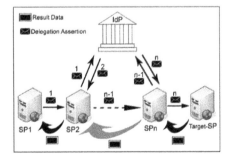

Figure 8.10: Handling delegation assertions in the indirect delegation model

Note that the target SP is always provided with information regarding the delegatee that forwarded the delegation assertion to it, since this information is included in the delegation assertion itself (i.e. in the `<Subject>` element). This means that if the user has requested that the result data must be encrypted, then every target SP must encrypt the data using the public key of the delegatee (or the delegation assertion subject) from which it received the delegation assertion. If an SP has acted as both target SP and delegatee in the same working session, then it must first decrypt the received result data using its private key before re-encrypting the data using the public key of the delegatee from which it received the delegation assertion.

Finally, although indirect delegation is supported, the proposed delegation system is not fully recursive since the protocol interactions for direct delegation are different to those for indirect delegation.

8.4.2   Delegation Assertion Revocation

Another important issue is revocation of delegations. The user may at any time wish to revoke a delegation, e.g. for security or operational reasons. In the case of indirect delegation, revoking a delegation by the user means revoking all the consequent delegation steps, even if the user might not be aware of them.

To meet this requirement, a *revocation list* can be implemented, containing the IDs of all withdrawn delegation assertions. Each IdP acting as a delegation authority will be responsible for publishing and updating such a list. A user wishing to revoke a delegation request makes a revocation request to the appropriate IdP. The IdP will authenticate the request, and, if the authentication succeeds, will add the revoked assertion to the revocation list. If this addition is made to the scheme, then a target SP will be required to check the status of every assertion before accepting it.

The SAML specifications do not address revocation, because assertions are intended to be used in short-term transactions. Nevertheless constructing a revocation list for SAML assertions would appear to be straightforward. As shown in figure 8.5, an assertion must include an element called `<Assertion>`, which has a number of attributes. The *ID* attribute holds a unique identifier for the assertion (there is only a negligible probability that another party will accidentally assign the same identifier to a different assertion [40]), and the *IssueInstant* attribute holds the time of issue of the assertion. These two attributes can be used to build a revocation table along the lines of table 8.1.

Table 8.1: Example of a revocation table

Assertion ID	Issuance time	Issued for
1120g447Cv9	2010-01-16T00:18:05Z	SP1.com
bv56548GGH3	2010-01-15T00:23:24Z	SP2.com
4tr6472SpO0	2010-01-14T00:08:18Z	SP3.com

In order to preserve user privacy, the table must contain no information about the users to which the delegations apply. Omitting the 'issuance time' and 'issued for' information from the table would be possible. However, including this information seems unlikely to raise serious privacy issues, especially since the existence of a federation relationship between an IdP and an SP is unlikely to be confidential.

8.4.3   Privacy

The level of privacy provided by the delegation scheme depends on the privacy features provided by the Liberty ID-WSF SAML 2.0 SSO profiles specifications. The unlinkability property is preserved by encrypting the Liberty-defined pseudonyms within a delegation assertion. Moreover, explicit user consent for the delegation process is mandatory, and the resulting data can be encrypted if the user so requests.

8.5   Related Work

As described in Section 4.8.2.3, the notion of extending the attribute statements in SAML in order to support delegation has been discussed previously by a number of authors. However, unlike the framework proposed here, previous schemes are generic (i.e. not designed specifically for Liberty), do not assume trust relationships between the system parties, and do not take into consideration the existing communication profiles for SAML 2.0 and Liberty. There are also a number of differences in the delegation assertion structure and in the message flows between the scheme described in this chapter and the systems listed in Section 4.8.2.3.

There are also a number of differences between the scheme described in this chapter and the Shibboleth delegation framework (see Section 4.8.2.1). For example, the Shibboleth delegation framework does not support the use of delegation assertions, does not support indirect delegation, and is not built on the SAML SSO profiles. As stated in Section 4.8.2.1, the Shibboleth delegation framework is built on a quite different concept which we refer to as 'user masquerading'.

In late 2009 OASIS[2] published its finalised specifications for SAML delegation assertions [45]. These specifications are rather brief, and focus on the structure of the delegation assertion rather than describing a complete delegation system.

Finally we note that the Sun[3] One Identity Server product, which implements the Liberty specifications, supports delegation. However, details of its delegation system do not appear to have been published.

---

[2]http://www.oasis-open.org
[3]http://www.sun.com

8.6   Conclusions

In this chapter we have proposed a delegation system for Liberty based on the ID-WSF SAML 2.0 SSO profiles. The scheme extends the attribute statements defined for a SAML assertion to include delegation-related information, and assumes that the target SP is capable of understanding the syntax and semantics of the delegated roles. It is designed to support both direct and indirect delegation, can be readily integrated into the currently deployed Liberty specifications, and preserves the privacy protection measures built into Liberty. We have also discussed a number of related issues, including an approach to providing support for revocation of delegations.

The scheme proposed in this chapter can be adopted by any Federated identity management system that is built on the SAML 2.0 SSO profiles. Providing support for delegation helps to enhance the practicality of a Federated identity management system.

One possible disadvantage of the proposed scheme is that it is designed to work only with identity management systems built on SAML 2.0 SSO profiles. Other systems, for example CardSpace, cannot adopt such a scheme. Another disadvantage is that the proposed indirect delegation model is not fully recursive.

Part III

Conclusions

Conclusions

Contents

This chapter summarises and concludes the thesis. After summarising the contributions of the thesis in section 9.1, in section 9.2 we discuss possible future work directed at enhancing the functionality and security properties of identity management systems.

9.1   Summary and Conclusions

The first part of this thesis is intended to provide the reader with the required background information and a review of the relevant literature.

In Chapter 2 we provided a brief introduction to the security services and mechanisms used throughout the thesis. We then, in Chapter 3, reviewed the concepts of identity and identity management, and introduce certain identity management models. Chapter 4 provides descriptions of the frameworks of five of the most widely discussed identity management systems, namely CardSpace, Higgins, Liberty, Shibboleth, and OpenID. It also describes certain security limitations shared by those systems, and reviews previous work aimed at enhancing the practicality of these systems by supporting interoperation and delegation.

In the second part of the thesis (consisting of chapters 5 8) we outlined a number of security vulnerabilities and practicality issues arising in web-based identity management systems. Novel schemes to enhance both the privacy and practicality of these systems have been proposed. The proposed schemes can be readily integrated with the current specifications of the relevant systems.

Chapters 5 and 6 address certain privacy threats arising in ICIM systems. In Chapter 5 we focused on two security vulnerabilities common to all systems, namely their reliance on the user's judgement on the authenticity of the SP and their reliance on a single layer of authentication. A scheme using Secured from Identity Theft (SIT) attributes was proposed to address these vulnerabilities. This scheme may be vulnerable to guessing attacks; we therefore also proposed a variety of measures to mitigate the risk of such attacks. Other possible ways of addressing the outlined vulnerabilities were also discussed. Two of these approaches are based on the use of proof-key services.

In Chapter 6 we proposed two methods to enhance user authentication in ICIM systems. The first method requires a user to perform an additional step before the SP completes the authentication process. That is, the user must present to the SP certain information sent to the user by the SP during the most recent successful use of the scheme. A proof-of-concept implementation of this method has been developed and was described. The second method involves a challenge-response exchange between the user and the SP. These methods provide the SP with an implicit indication that log-in attempts have been initiated by legitimate users. Implementing these methods would help to enhance the accuracy of the SP judgement of the legitimacy of the user. Since the schemes mitigate the threat of an IdP impersonating its users, they should help to make ICIM systems more acceptable to end users.

Chapters 7 and 8 describe techniques designed to enhance the practicality of both Information Card-based and Federated identity management systems. In Chapter 7 we proposed a scheme enabling interoperation between Liberty and CardSpace. This helps to enhance their practicality, and could be of major benefit to both the users and implementers of these systems. The scheme takes advantage of the similarities between the Liberty ID-WSF SAML SSO LEC profile and the CardSpace message flows. The scheme uses a client-side identity management architecture adaptor, that converts the format of messages within the message flows of the two systems. The scheme is designed to enable interoperation between two identity management systems with somewhat different scopes, and this has led to certain technical problems. We have proposed possible solutions to these problems. A description of a prototype implementation of the proposed integration model has also been provided.

In Chapter 8 we proposed a delegation framework for Liberty based on SAML 2.0 and the Liberty ID-FF 1.2 SSO profiles. The delegation scheme extends the attribute statements defined for a SAML assertion to contain delegation-related information, and supports both direct and indirect delegation. We also discussed a number of related issues, including the provision of a revocation method for delegation assertions. The delegation scheme preserves the Liberty privacy protection measures, and can be adopted by any Federated identity management system built on the SAML 2.0 SSO profiles. Implementation of this delegation scheme will help to enhance the practicality of Federated identity management systems.

9.2   Possible Future Work

We conclude the thesis by discussing possible future work directed at enhancing the functionality and security properties of identity management systems.

It seems likely that a Proof-of-Authenticity method similar to that proposed in Section 6.3.1 can also be used in Federated identity management systems. However, in the most commonly adopted SSO profiles of the Liberty ID-FF (i.e. the Artifact and Browser POST profiles), there is no need for an enabling component to be installed on the user machine, since the IdP and the SP can communicate directly [177]. This means that methods similar to those proposed in section 6.3.2 would not be appropriate for Liberty and probably many other Federated identity management systems.

Another possible direction for future work would involve enhancing user authentication in Federated identity management systems by distributing user trust across multiple trusted parties (or trust brokers), e.g. by requiring the use of two or more IdPs. Such an approach might involve a user agent presenting to the SP a 'Proof-of-Authenticity assertion' issued and signed by one or more trusted parties (e.g. IdPs), along with the authentication assertion. Before issuing the Proof-of-Authenticity assertion assertion, a trusted party might be required to obtain explicit approval from the user. This would mitigate the risk of an IdP impersonating its users.

Bibliography

[1] OECD guidelines on the protection of privacy and transborder flows of personal data. Organisation for Economic Co-operation and Development, September 1980.

[2] Guide to Sun Microsystems Java Plug-in Security, report number C43-022R-2003, December 2003. Network Applications Team of the Systems and Network Attack Center (SNAC), National Security Agency (NSA), USA.

[3] At a crossroads: "personhood" and digital identity in the information society. Organisation for Economic Co-operation and Development, February 2008.

[4] Mapping IDABC Authentication Assurance Levels to SAML v2.0 — Gap analysis and recommendations, November 2008. ENISA Report.

[5] Martín Abadi, Michael Burrows, Butler Lampson, and Gordon Plotkin. A calculus for access control in distributed systems. *ACM Transactions on Programming Languages and Systems*, 15(4):706–734, 1993.

[6] Gail-Joon Ahn, Moonam Ko, and Mohamed Shehab. Portable user-centric identity management. In *Proceedings of the IFIP TC-11 23rd International Information Security Conference, IFIP 20th World Computer Congress, IFIP SEC 2008, Milano, Italy*, pages 573–587. Springer-Verlag, 2008.

[7] Mehran Ahsant, Jim Basney, and Olle Mulmo. Grid delegation protocol. Technical Report YCS-2004-380, University of York, Department of Computer Science, July 2004.

[8] Haitham S. Al-Sinani, Waleed A. Alrodhan, and Chris J. Mitchell. CardSpace-Liberty integration for CardSpace users. In *Proceedings of the 9th Symposium on Identity and Trust on the Internet, IDtrust 2010, Gaithersburg, Maryland, USA, April 13-15, 2010*, pages 12–25. ACM, 2010.

[9] W. A. Alrodhan and C. J. Mitchell. Addressing privacy issues in CardSpace. In *Proceedings of the Third International Symposium on Information Assurance and Security, IAS 2007, Manchester, UK*, pages 285–291. IEEE Computer Society, 2007.

[10] W. A. Alrodhan and C. J. Mitchell. A client-side CardSpace-Liberty integration architecture. In *Proceedings of the Seventh symposium on Identity and trust on the Internet , IDTrust 2008, NIST, Gaithersburg, USA*, volume 283, pages 1–7. ACM International Conference Proceeding Series, 2008.

[11] W. A. Alrodhan and C. J. Mitchell. A delegation framework for Liberty. In *Proceedings of the Third Conference on Advances in Computer Securityand Forensics, ACSF 2008, Liverpool, UK*, pages 67–73. Liverpool John Moores University, 2008.

[12] W. A. Alrodhan and C. J. Mitchell. Improving the security of CardSpace. *EURASIP Journal on Information Security*, 9, 2009. Article ID 167216.

[13] W. A. Alrodhan and C. J. Mitchell. Enhancing user authentication in claim-based identity management. In *Proceedings of the 2010 International Symposium on Collaborative Technologies and Systems, CTS 2010, Chicago, Illinois, USA*, pages 75–83. IEEE, 2010.

[14] R. Arends, R. Austein, M. Larson, D. Massey, and S. Rose. DNS security introduction and requirements. RFC 4033, Internet Engineering Task Force, March 2005.

[15] Alapan Arnab and Andrew Hutchison. Persistent access control: A formal model for DRM. In *Proceedings of the ACM workshop on Digital Rights Management, DRM 2007*, pages 41–53, New York, NY, USA, 2007. ACM.

[16] Mark Atwood, Richard M. Conlan, Blaine Cook, Leah Culver, Kellan Elliott-McCrea, Larry Halff, Eran Hammer-Lahav, Ben Laurie, Chris Messina, John Panzer, Sam Quigley, David Recordon, Eran Sandler, Jonathan Sergent, Todd Sieling, Brian Slesinsky, and Andy Smith. OAuth Core 1.0. http://oauth.net/core/1.0, December 2007. OAuth Core Workgroup.

[17] P. Austel, S. Bhola, S. Chari, L. Koved, M. McIntosh, M. Steiner, and S. Weber. Secure Delegation for Web 2.0 and Mashups. A Position Statement for the 2008 Workshop on Web 2.0 Security and Privacy (W2SP), 2008. IBM Corporation.

[18] Olav L. Bandmann, Babak Sadighi Firozabadi, and Mads Dam. Constrained delegation. In *Proceedings of the 2002 IEEE Symposium on Security and Privacy*, pages 131–140. IEEE Computer Society, 2002.

[19] T. Berners-Lee, R. Fielding, and L. Masinter. Uniform resource identifier (uri): Generic syntax. RFC 3986, Internet Engineering Task Force, January 2005.

[20] Vittorio Bertocci, Garrett Serack, and Caleb Baker. *Understanding Windows CardSpace*. Addison-Wesley, 2008.

[21] Konstantin Beznosov, Donald J. Flinn, Shirley Kawamoto, and Bret Hartman. Introduction to Web services and their security. *Information Security Technical Report*, 10:2–14, 2005.

[22] Abhilasha Bhargav-Spantzel, Annna C. Squicciarini, and Elisa Bertino. Establishing and protecting digital identity in federation systems. In *Proceedings of the 2005 Workshop on Digital Identity Management, Fairfax, VA, USA, November 11, 2005*, pages 11–19. ACM, 2005.

[23] Joshua B. Bolten (director). E-Authentication Guidance for Federal Agencies — M-04-04, December 2003. Office of Management and Budget (OMB), Executive Office of the President, The White House, Washington DC, USA.

[24] David Booth, Hugo Haas, Francis McCabe, Eric Newcomer, Michael Champion, Chris Ferris, and David Orchard (editors). Web services architecture, February 2004. The World Wide Web Consortium (W3C).

[25] Don Box and Francisco Curbera (editors). Web services addressing (ws-addressing), August 2004. The World Wide Web Consortium (W3C).

[26] R. Braden (editor). Requirements for internet hosts — communication layers. RFC 1122, Internet Engineering Task Force, October 1989.

[27] Pete Bramhall, Marit Hansen, Kai Rannenberg, and Thomas Roessler. User-centric identity management: New trends in standardization and regulation. *IEEE Security & Privacy*, 5(4):84–87, July/August 2007.

[28] Johnny Bufu and Jonathan Daugherty (editors). OpenID Provider Authentication Policy Extension 1.0. http://openid.net/specs/openid-provider-authentication-policy-extension-1_0.html, December 2008. The OpenID Foundation.

[29] William E. Burr, Donna F. Dodson, and W. Timothy Polk. Electronic Authentication Guideline — Special Publication 800-63 — Version 1.0.2, April 2006. Recommendations of the National Institute of Standards and Technology (NIST), USA.

[30] CA/Browser forum. Guidelines for the issuance and management of extended validation certificates — version 1.1, April 2008.

[31] Conor Cahill and Jeff Hodges (editors). Liberty ID-WSF web services discovery service specification — version: 2.0, 2006. Liberty Alliance Project.

[32] Jan Camenisch, Abhi Shelat, Dieter Sommer, Simone Fischer-Hübner, Marit Hansen, Henry Krasemann, Gérard Lacoste, Ronald Leenes, and Jimmy C. Tseng. Privacy and identity management for everyone. In *Proceedings of the 2005 Workshop on Digital Identity Management*, pages 20–27, Fairfax, VA, USA, November 2005. ACM.

[33] Kim Cameron. The laws of identity, May 2005. Microsoft Corporation.

[34] Kim Cameron and Michael B. Jones. Design rationale behind the identity metasystem architecture, February 2006. Microsoft Corporation.

[35] Scott Cantor. User Authentication and Subject Identifiers in Shibboleth. https://spaces.internet2.edu/display/SHIB/IdPUserAuthnConfig, June.

[36] Scott Cantor. Attribute Release Policies. https://spaces.internet2.edu/display/SHIB/IdPARPConfig, January 2008. Internet2.

[37] Scott Cantor, Frederick Hirsch, John Kemp, Rob Philpott, and Eve Maler (editors). Bindings for the OASIS Security Assertion Markup Language (SAML) V2.0, March 2005. OASIS Standard Specification, OASIS Open.

[38] Scott Cantor and Michael B. Jones (editors). SAML V2.0 Information Card Token Profile — version 1.0 — CD 03, July 2010. OASIS Standard Specification, OASIS Open.

[39] Scott Cantor, John Kemp, and Darryl Champagne (editors). Liberty ID-FF bindings and profiles specification — 1.2-errata-v2.0, 2004. Liberty Alliance Project.

[40] Scott Cantor, John Kemp, Rob Philpott, and Eve Maler (editors). Assertions and Protocols for the OASIS Security Assertion Markup Language (SAML) V2.0, March 2005. OASIS Standard Specification, OASIS Open.

[41] Scott Cantor and John Kemp (editors). Liberty ID-FF Protocols and Schema Specification — 1.2-errata-v3.0, 2004. Liberty Alliance Project.

[42] Scott Cantor, Jahan Moreh, Rob Philpott, and Eve Maler (editors). Metadata for the OASIS Security Assertion Markup Language (SAML) V2.0, March 2005. OASIS Standard Specification, OASIS Open.

[43] Scott Cantor (editor). SAML 2.0 single sign-on with constrained delegation. http://shibboleth.internet2.edu/shibboleth-documents.html, October 2005. Internet2.

[44] Scott Cantor (editor). Shibboleth Architecture — Protocols and Profiles. http://shibboleth.internet2.edu/docs/internet2-mace-shibboleth-arch-protocols-200509.pdf, September 2005. Internet2.

[45] Scott Cantor (editor). SAML V2.0 Condition for Delegation Restriction Version 1.0, November 2009. OASIS Standard Specification, OASIS Open.

[46] David W. Chadwick. Delegation issuing service for x.509. In *Proceedings of the 4th Annual PKI R&D Workshop, USA*, volume IR 7224, pages 66–77. NIST Technical Publication, April 2005.

[47] David W. Chadwick. Federated identity management. In Alessandro Aldini, Gilles Barthe, and Roberto Gorrieri, editors, *Foundations of Security Analysis and Design V, FOSAD 2007/2008/2009 Tutorial Lectures*, volume 5705 of *Lecture Notes in Computer Science*, pages 96–120. Springer, 2008.

[48] David W. Chadwick and George Inman. Attribute aggregation in federated identity management. *IEEE Computer*, 42(5):33–40, 2009.

[49] David W. Chadwick, Sassa Otenko, and Tuan Anh Nguyen. Adding support to XACML for multi-domain user to user dynamic delegation of authority. *International Journal of Information Security*, 8:137–152, 2009.

[50] Erik Christensen, Francisco Curbera, Greg Meredith, and Sanjiva Weerawarana. Web Services Description Language (WSDL) — version 1.1, March 2001. The World Wide Web Consortium (W3C).

[51] Sebastian Claubeta, Dogan Kesdogan, and Tobias Kölsch. Privacy enhancing identity management: protection against re-identification and profiling. In *Proceedings of the the 2005 Workshop on Digital Identity Management, Fairfax, VA, USA*, pages 84–93. ACM, 2005.

[52] John Henry Clippinger. Higgins Towards a Foundation Layer for the Social Web. Higgins — working draft, December 2009.

[53] Jason Crampton and Hemanth Khambhammettu. Delegation in role-based access control. *International Journal of Information Security (IJIS)*, 7(2):123–136, 2008.

[54] Francisco Curbera, Savas Parastatidis, and Jeffrey Schlimmer (editors). Web services metadata exchange (WS-MetadataExchange) — version 1.1, August 2006. BEA Systems, Computer Associates, IBM, Microsoft, SAP AG, Sun Microsystems, and webMethods.

[55] Russ Cutler (editor). Liberty Identity Assurance Framework — version 1.1, 2008. Liberty Alliance Project.

[56] Alexander W. Dent and Chris J. Mitchell. *User's Guide to Cryptography and Standards*. Artech House, London, UK, 2004.

[57] T. Dierks and C. Allen. The TLS protocol — version 1.0. RFC 2246, Internet Engineering Task Force, January 1999.

[58] T. Dierks and E. Rescorla. The transport layer security (TLS) protocol — version 1.1. RFC 4346, Internet Engineering Task Force, April 2006.

[59] Whitfield Diffie and Martin E. Hellman. New Directions in Cryptograph. *IEEE Transactions on Information Theory*, IT-22(6):644–654, November 1976.

[60] M. Duerst and M. Suignard. Internationalized resource identifiers (iris). RFC 3987, Internet Engineering Task Force, January 2005.

[61] D. Eastlake and P. Jones. US secure hash algorithm 1 (SHA1). RFC 3174, Internet Engineering Task Force, September 2001.

[62] Donald Eastlake, Joseph Reagle, and David Solo (editors). XML-Signature syntax and processing, February 2002. The World Wide Web Consortium (W3C).

[63] Donald Eastlake and Joseph Reagle (editors). XML-Encryption syntax and processing, December 2002. The World Wide Web Consortium (W3C).

[64] Gary Ellison (editor). Liberty ID-WSF security mechanisms — version: 1.2, 2005. Liberty Alliance Project.

[65] U. Feige, A. Fiat, and A. Shamir. Zero knowledge proofs of identity. In *Proceedings of the 19th Annual ACM Symposium on Theory of Computing, 1987, New York, NY*, pages 210–217. ACM, 1987.

[66] Warwick Ford. *Computer Communications Security*. Prentice-Hall, Englewood Cliffs, NJ, USA, 1994.

[67] Warwick Ford and Michael S. Baum. *Secure Electronic Commerce: Building the Infrastructure for Digital Signatures & Encryption*. Prentice Hall PTR, Upper Saddle River, New Jersey, USA, 2001.

[68] Sebastian Gajek, Jörg Schwenk, and Chen Xuan. On the insecurity of Microsoft's identity metasystem. Technical Report TR-HGI-2008-003, Horst Görtz Institute for IT Security, Ruhr-Universität Bochum, June 2008.

[69] Taher El Gamal. A public key cryptosystem and a signature scheme based on discrete logarithms. In *Proceedings of CRYPTO '84, Santa Barbara, California, USA*, volume 196 of *Lecture Notes in Computer Science*, pages 10–18. Springer-Verlag, 1985.

[70] Simson Garfinkel. *PGP: Pretty Good Privacy*. O'Reilly Media, Inc., Sebastopol, CA, USA, 1994.

[71] Dieter Gollmann. *Computer Security*. John Wiley & Sons, 2004.

[72] Hidehito Gomi, Makoto Hatakeyama, Shigeru Hosono, and Satoru Fujita. A delegation framework for federated identity management. In *Proceedings of the workshop on digital identity management (DIM '05)*, pages 94–103, New York, NY, USA, 2005. ACM Press.

[73] Hans Graux and Jarkko Majava. eID Interoperability for PEGS — Proposal for a multi-level authentication mechanism and a mapping of existing authentication mechanisms, December 2007. The Interoperable Delivery of European eGovernment Services to public Administrations, Businesses and Citizens (IDABC).

[74] Eran Hammer-Lahav and Will Norris (editors). Extensible Resource Descriptor (XRD) Version 1.0 — Working Draft 10, November 2009. OASIS Open.

[75] Eran Hammer-Lahav (editors). OAuth Core 1.0 Revision A. http://oauth.net/core/1.0a, June 2009. OAuth Core Workgroup.

[76] D. Hardt, J. Bufu, and J. Hoyt. OpenID Attribute Exchange 1.0 — Final. http://openid.net/specs/openid-attribute-exchange-1_0.html, December 2007. The OpenID Foundation.

[77] Kipp E.B. Hickman. The SSL protocol. Netscape Communications Corp., February 1995.

[78] Jeff Hodges. Technical Comparison: OpenID and SAML — Draft 07a. http://identitymeme.org/doc/draft-hodges-saml-openid-compare-05.html, July 2009. Whitepaper, identitymeme.org.

[79] Jeff Hodges, Robert Aarts, Paul Madsen, and Scott Cantor (editors). Liberty ID-WSF Authentication, Single Sign-On, and Identity Mapping Services Specification — version: 2.0, 2006. Liberty Alliance Project.

[80] Jeff Hodges and Robert Aarts (editors). Liberty ID-WSF Authentication Service and Single Sign-On Service Specification — version: 1.1, 2005. Liberty Alliance Project.

[81] Arnaud Le Hors, Philippe Le Hégaret, Lauren Wood, Gavin Nicol, Jonathan Robie, Mike Champion, and Steve Byrne (editors). Document object model (dom) level 2 core specification — version 1.0, November 2000. The World Wide Web Consortium (W3C).

[82] John Hughes, Scott Cantor, Jeff Hodges, Frederick Hirsch, Prateek Mishra, Rob Philpott, and Eve Maler (editors). Profiles for the OASIS Security Assertion Markup Language (SAML) V2.0, March 2005. OASIS Standard Specification, OASIS Open.

[83] Phil Hunt (editor). Client Attribute Requirements Markup Language (CARML) Specification — Working draft 03, 2006. Oracle.

[84] International Organization for Standardization. *ISO 7498-2: Information processing systems — Open Systems Interconnection — Basic Reference Model — Part 2: Security Architecture*, 1989.

[85] International Organization for Standardization. *ISO/IEC 10118-4: Information technology — Security techniques — Hash Functions — Part 4: Hash-functions using modular arithmetic*, 1994.

[86] International Organization for Standardization. *ISO/IEC 9797-1: Information technology — Security techniques — Message Authentication Codes (MACs) — Part 1: Mechanisms using a block cipher*, 1999.

[87] International Organization for Standardization. *ISO/IEC 10118-1: Information technology — Security techniques — Hash Functions — Part 1: General*, 2000.

[88] International Organization for Standardization. *ISO/IEC 10118-2: Information technology — Security techniques — Hash Functions — Part 2: Hash-functions using an n-bit block cipher*, 2000.

[89] International Organization for Standardization. *ISO/IEC 9796-2: Information technology — Security techniques — Digital signature schemes giving message recovery — Part 2: Integer factorization based mechanisms*, 2002.

[90] International Organization for Standardization. *ISO/IEC 9797-2: Information technology — Security techniques — Message Authentication Codes (MACs) — Part 2: Mechanisms using a dedicated hash-function*, June 2002.

[91] International Organization for Standardization. *ISO/IEC 10118-3: Information technology — Security techniques — Hash Functions — Part 3: Dedicated hash functions*, 2004.

[92] International Organization for Standardization. *ISO/IEC 9798-5: Information technology — Security techniques — Entity authentication — Part 5: Mechanisms using zero-knowledge techniques*, 2004.

[93] International Organization for Standardization. *ISO/IEC 18033-3: Information technology — Security techniques — Encryption algorithms — Part 3: Block ciphers*, 2005.

[94] International Organization for Standardization. *ISO/IEC 18033-4: Information technology — Security techniques — Encryption algorithms — Part 4: Stream ciphers*, 2005.

[95] International Organization for Standardization. *ISO/IEC 14888-3: Information technology — Security techniques — Digital signatures with appendix — Part 3: Discrete logarithm based mechanisms*, 2006.

[96] International Organization for Standardization. *ISO/IEC 18033-2: Information technology — Security techniques — Encryption algorithms — Part 2: Asymmetric ciphers*, May 2006.

[97] International Organization for Standardization. *ISO/IEC 9796-3: Information technology — Security techniques — Digital signature schemes giving message recovery — Part 3: Discrete logarithm based mechanisms*, 2006.

[98] International Organization for Standardization. *ISO/IEC 14888-1: Information technology — Security techniques — Digital signatures with appendix — Part 1: General*, 2008.

[99] International Organization for Standardization. *ISO/IEC 14888-2: Information technology — Security techniques — Digital signatures with appendix — Part 2: Integer factorization based mechanisms*, 2008.

[100] International Organization for Standardization. *ISO/IEC 13888-1: Information technology — Security techniques — Non-repudiation — Part 1: General*, 2009.

[101] International Organization for Standardization, Genève, Switzerland. *ISO/IEC Second CD 24760 — Information technology — Security techniques — A framework for identity management*, January 2010.

[102] International Telecommunication Union — Telecommunication Standardization Sector (ITU-T). *Y.2720 (Y.ngnIdMframework), NGN Identity management framework — Draft Recommendation*, September 2008.

[103] International Telecommunication Union — Telecommunication Standardization Sector (ITU-T). *ITU-T X.1250 (X.idmreq), Baseline capabilities for enhanced global identity management trust and interoperability — Draft new Recommendation*, February 2009.

[104] International Telecommunication Union. *X.509 Information technology — Open Systems Interconnection — The Directory: Public-key and attribute certificate frameworks*, 2000.

[105] International Telecommunication Union. *X.680 Information technology — Abstract Syntax Notation One (ASN.1): Specification of basic notation*, 2002.

[106] International Telecommunication Union. *X.509 Information technology — Open Systems Interconnection — The Directory: Public-key and attribute certificate frameworks*, 2005.

[107] Chad La Joie (editor). WS-Trust 1.3 Interoperability Profile — Working Draft 01, January 2008. SWITCH.

[108] Michael B. Jones. A guide to supporting InfoCard v1.0 within web applications and browsers, March 2006. Microsoft Corporation.

[109] Mike Jones, Ross MacIntyre, Terry Morrow, Aleksandra Nenadić, Stephen Pickles, and Ning Zhang. E-infrastructure Security: Levels of Assurance, November 2006. The Joint Information Systems Committee (JISC).

[110] Ivar Jørstada, Do van Thuan, Tore Jønvikc, and Do van Thanh. Bridging CardSpace and Liberty Alliance with SIM authentication. In *Proceedings of the 10th International Conference on Intelligence in Next Generation Networks, ICIN 2007, Bordeaux, France*, pages 8–13. ADERA, 2007.

[111] Audun Jøsang and Simon Pope. User centric identity management. In *Proceedings of Australian Computer Emergency Response Team Conference (AusCERT 2005)*, 2005.

[112] Audun Jøsang, Mohammed Al Zomai, and Suriadi Suriadi. Usability and privacy in identity management architectures. In *Proceedings of the Fifth Australasian Information Security Workshop (Privacy Enhancing Technologies) (AISW 2007), Victoria, Australia*, pages 143–152. Australian Computer Society, 2007.

[113] Sampo Kellomai (editor). Liberty ID-SIS employee profile service specification — version: 1.0, 2003. Liberty Alliance Project.

[114] John Kemp, Scott Cantor, Prateek Mishra, Rob Philpott, and Eve Maler (editors). Authentication Context for the OASIS Security Assertion Markup Language (SAML) V2.0, March 2005. OASIS Open.

[115] S. Kent and K. Seo. Security architecture for the internet protocol. RFC 4301, Internet Engineering Task Force, December 2005.

[116] Seung Hyun Kim, Dae Seon Choi, Deok Jin Kim, Soo Hyung Kim, Jong Hyouk Noh, Kwan Soo Jung, Sang Rea Cho, Young Seob Cho, Jin Man Cho, and Seung Hun Jin. OpenID Authentication Method Using Identity Selector. United States Patent, October 2009. US 2009/0249078 A1.

[117] Marc Langheinrich (editor). A P3P Preference Exchange Language 1.0 (AP-PEL1.0) — Working Draft, April 2002. The World Wide Web Consortium (W3C).

[118] Paul Madsen (editor). Liberty ID-WSF People Service — federated social identity, December.

[119] Paul Madsen (editor). Liberty IGF Privacy Constraints Specification — version 1.0-04, 2008. Liberty Alliance Project.

[120] Eve Maler, Prateek Mishra, and Rob Philpott (editors). Assertions and Protocol for the OASIS Security Assertion Markup Language (SAML) V1.1, September 2003. OASIS Standard Specification, OASIS Open.

[121] Eve Maler, Prateek Mishra, and Robert Philpott (editors). Bindings and Profiles for the OASIS Security Assertion Markup Language (SAML) V1.1, September 2003. OASIS Standard Specification, OASIS Open.

[122] Alfred J. Menezes, Paul C. Van Oorschot, and Scott A. Vanstone. *Handbook of Applied Cryptography.* CRC Press, FL, USA, 1997.

[123] Microsoft Corporation. Microsoft's vision for an identity metasystem, May 2005.

[124] Microsoft Corporation. A technical reference for InfoCard v1.0 in windows, August 2005.

[125] Microsoft Corporation. A Guide to Using the Identity Selector Interoperability Profile V1.5 within Web Applications and Browsers, July 2008.

[126] Microsoft Corporation and Ping Identity Corporation. A guide to integrating with InfoCard v1.0, August 2005.

[127] Joaquin   Miller   (editor).   Yadis   1.0   (HTML). http://yadis.org/wiki/Yadis_1.0_%28HTML%29, March 2006.   The Identity and Accountability Foundation for Web 2.0.

[128] Prateek Mishra (editor). AAPML: Attribute Authority Policy Markup Language — Working Draft 08, 2006. Oracle.

[129] Nilo Mitra and Yves Lafon (editors). SOAP — version 1.2, April 2007. The World Wide Web Consortium (W3C).

[130] Ronald Monzillo, Chris Kaler, Anthony Nadalin, and Phillip Hallem-Baker (editors). Web Services Security: SAML Token Profile 1.1, February 2006. OASIS Standard Specification, OASIS Open.

[131] Bob Morgan, Scott Cantor, Steven Carmody Walter Hoehn, and Ken Klingenstein. Federated Security: The Shibboleth Approach. *EDUCAUSE Quarterly*, 27(4):12–17, 2004.

[132] SangYeob Na and SuhHyun Cheon. Role delegation in role-based access control. In *Proceedings of the fifth ACM workshop on Role-based access control (RBAC '00)*, pages 39–44, New York, NY, USA, 2000. ACM.

[133] Anthony Nadalin, Marc Goodner, Martin Gudgin, Abbie Barbir, and Hans Granqvist (editors). WS-SecurityPolicy — version 1.2, July 2007. OASIS Standard.

[134] Anthony Nadalin, Marc Goodner, Martin Gudgin, Abbie Barbir, and Hans Granqvist (editors). WS-Trust — version 1.3, March 2007. OASIS Standard.

[135] Anthony Nadalin, Chris Kaler, Ronald Monzillo, and Phillip Hallam-Baker (editors). Web services security: SOAP message security — version 1.1, February 2006. OASIS Standard Specification.

[136] Anthony Nadalin and Chris Kaler (editors). Web services federation language WS-Federation, version 1.1, December 2006. BEA Systems, BMC Software, CA, IBM, Layer 7 Technologies, Microsoft, Novell, and VeriSign.

[137] Arun Nanda. Identity selector interoperability profile v1.0, April 2007. Microsoft Corporation.

[138] Andrew Nash, William Duane, Celia Joseph, and Derek Brink. *PKI: Implementing and Managing E-security*. Osborne/McGraw-Hill, 2001.

[139] National Institute of Standards and Technology, Gaithersburg, MD, USA. *FIPS PUB 197: Advanced Encryption Standard (AES)*, November 2001.

[140] National Institute of Standards and Technology, Gaithersburg, MD, USA. *Security Requirements for Cryptographic Modules*, May 2001.

[141] National Institute of Standards and Technology, Gaithersburg, MD, USA. *FIPS PUB 198: The Keyed-Hash Message Authentication Code (HMAC)*, March 2002.

[142] National Institute of Standards and Technology, Gaithersburg, MD, USA. *FIPS PUB 180-2: Secure Hash Standard*, February 2004.

[143] Guillermo Navarro, Babak Sadighi Firozabadi, Erik Rissanen, and Joan Borrell. Constrained delegation in XML-based access control and digital rights management standards. In *Proceedings of IASTED Conference on Communication, Network and Information Security, CNIS 2003*, New York, NY, USA, 2003. Acta Press.

[144] Nadia Nedjah and Luiza De Macedo Mourelle (editors). *Embedded Cryptographic Hardware: Design & Security*. Nova Science Publishers, 2006.

[145] T. Negrino and D. Smith. *JavaScript and Ajax for the Web: Visual QuickStart Guide*. Peachpit Press, Berkeley, CA, USA, 2008.

[146] Arshad Noor. Identity protection factor (ipf). In *The 7th Symposium on Identity and Trust on the Internet (IDtrust 2008)*, volume 283 of *International Conference Proceeding Series*, pages 8–18. ACM, 2008.

[147] Andreas Pfitzmann and Marit Köhntopp. Anonymity, unobservability, and pseudonymity — a proposal for terminology. In *Proceedings of Designing Privacy Enhancing Technologies: International Workshop on Design Issues in Anonymity and Unobservability, Berkeley, CA, USA*, volume 2009 of Lecture Notes in Computer Science, pages 1–9. Springer-Verlag, Berlin, Germany, July 2000.

[148] Quan Pham, Jason Reid, Adrian McCullagh, and Edward Dawson. On a taxonomy of delegation. *Computers & Security*, 29(5):565–579, July 2010.

[149] T. A. Powell and F. Schneider. *Javascript: The Complete Reference.* McGraw-Hill Osborne Media, Berkeley, CA, USA, 2004.

[150] David Recordon, Johnny Bufu, and Josh Hoyt (editors). OpenID Authentication 2.0. http://openid.net/specs/openid-authentication-2_0.html, December 2007. The OpenID Foundation.

[151] Drummond Reed and Dave McAlpin (editors). Extensible Resource Identifier (XRI) Syntax V2.0, November 2005. OASIS Open.

[152] E. Rescorla. Diffie-hellman key agreement method. RFC 2631, Internet Engineering Task Force, June 1999.

[153] Ronald L. Rivest, M.J.B. Robshaw, R. Sidney, and Y.L. Yin. *The RC6 Block Cipher, Version 1.1.* RSA Security, August 1998.

[154] Ronald L. Rivest, Adi Shamir, and Leonard Adleman. A method for obtaining digital signatures and public-key cryptosystems. Technical Report MIT/LCS/TM-82, MIT, 1977.

[155] Ronald L. Rivest, Adi Shamir, and Leonard Adleman. A method for obtaining digital signatures and public-key cryptosystems. *Commun. ACM*, 21(2):120–126, 1978.

[156] RNCOS. *Identity and Access Management Market Forecast to 2012 (research report)*, February 2009. http://www.rncos.com/Report/IM181.htm.

[157] M. Sabadello, P. Trevithick, and D. Reed. Universal data identifiers. Parity Communications Inc., April 2009.

[158] Manuel Sánchez, Óscar Cánovas Reverte, Gabriel López, and Antonio F. Gómez-Skarmeta. Managing the lifecycle of XACML delegation policies in federated environments. In *Proceedings of The IFIP TC-11 23rd International Information Security Conference, IFIP 20th World Computer Congress, IFIP SEC 2008, Milano, Italy*, pages 717–721. Springer-Verlag, 2008.

[159] Tom Scavo (editor). SAML V2.0 Holder-of-Key Assertion Profile — Version 1.0 — Committee Draft 3, November 2009. OASIS Open.

[160] Bruce Schneier. *Cryptography: Protocols, Algorithms, and Source Code in C.* John Wiley & Sons, Inc., New York, NY, 1996.

[161] Claus Peter Schnorr. Efficient identification and signatures for smart cards. In Gilles Brassard, editor, *Advances in Cryptology — CRYPTO '89: Proceedings of the ninth Annual International Cryptology Conference, Santa Barbara, California, USA*, volume 435 of *Lecture Notes in Computer Science*, pages 239–252. Springer-Verlag, 1990.

[162] Scott Seely. XML and Web Services Security: Understanding WS-Security, October 2002. Microsoft Corporation.

[163] Ludwig Seitz, Erik Rissanen, Thomas Sandholm, Babak Sadighi Firozabadi, and Olle Mulmo. Policy administration control and delegation using XACML and delegent. In *Proceedings of the 6th IEEE/ACM International Conference on Grid Computing, GRID 2005, Seattle, Washington, USA*, pages 49–54. IEEE, 2005.

[164] Nigel Smart. *Cryptography: An Introduction.* McGraw-Hill Education, Maidenhead, Berkshire UK, 2003.

[165] William Stallings. *Network Security Essentials: Applications and Standards.* Pearson Education, New Jersey, USA, 2008.

[166] Suriadi Suriadi, Ernest Foo, and Audun Jøsang. A user-centric federated single sign-on system. *Journal of Network and Computer Applications*, 32:388–401, 2009.

[167] Joan Van Tassel. *Digital Rights Management: Protecting and Monetizing Content.* Focal Press, 2006.

[168] John A. Taylor, Miriam Lips, and Joe Organ. Identification practices in government: citizen surveillance and the quest for public service improvement. *Identity in the Information Society*, 2009. Springer-Verlag.

[169] Stephen A. Thomas. *SSL and TLS Essentials: Securing the Web*. John Wiley & Sons, New York, USA, 2000.

[170] Peter Thompson and Darryl Champagne (editors). Liberty ID-FF implementation guidelines — version 1.2, 2004. Liberty Alliance Project.

[171] Eric Tiffany, Paul Madsen, and Scott Cantor (editors). Level of Assurance Authentication Context Profile for SAML 2.0 — Working Draft 03, May 2009. OASIS Open.

[172] Dobromir Todorov. *Mechanics of User Identification and Authentication: Fundamentals of Identity Management*. Auerbach Publications, 2007.

[173] Jonathan Tourzan and Yuzo Koga (editors). Liberty ID-WSF web services framework overview — version: 1.1. Liberty Alliance Project.

[174] Paul Trevithick. Relationship cards. Higgins Report 19 — Draft 0.46, September 2009.

[175] Gabe Wachob, Drummond Reed, Les Chasen, William Tan, and Steve Churchill (editors). Extensible Resource Identifier (XRI) Resolution Version 2.0 — Committee Draft 03, February 2008. OASIS Open.

[176] Jun Wang, David Del Vecchio, and Marty Humphrey. Extending the security assertion markup language to support delegation for web services and grid services. In *IEEE International Conference on Web Services (ICWS 2005)*, volume 1, pages 67–74. IEEE Computer Society, 2005.

[177] Thomas Wason (editor). Liberty ID-FF architecture overview — version: 1.2. Liberty Alliance Project.

[178] Yonghe Wei and Qilin Shu. A delegation-based workflow access control model. In *Proceedings of the The First International Symposium on Data, Privacy, and E-Commerce (ISDPE '07)*, pages 478–483, Washington, DC, USA, 2007. IEEE Computer Society.

[179] Rigo Wenning and Matthias Schunter (editors). The platform for privacy preferences — version 1.1. W3C Working Group Note, November 2006.

[180] Rod Widdowson and Scott Cantor (editors). Identity Provider Discovery Service Protocol and Profile — Committee Specification 01, March 2008. OASIS Standard Specification, OASIS Open.

[181] Phillip Windley. *Digital Identity.* O'Reilly Media, 2005.

[182] Sven Wohlgemuth and Günter Müller. Privacy with delegation of rights by identity management. In *Proceedings of the Emerging Trends in Information and Communication Security, International Conference (ETRICS 2006)*, volume 3995 of *Lecture Notes in Computer Science*, pages 175–190. Springer-Verlag, 2006.

[183] T. Ylonen and C. Lonvick (editor). The Secure Shell (SSH) protocol architecture. RFC 4251, Internet Engineering Task Force, January 2006.

[184] Longhua Zhang, Gail-Joon Ahn, and Bei-Tseng Chu. A rule-based framework for role based delegation. In *Proceedings of the sixth ACM symposium on Access control models and technologies (SACMAT '01)*, pages 153–162, New York, NY, USA, 2001. ACM.

Part IV

Appendix

Source Code for the Proof-of-consent Method

This appendix contains the source code for the proof-of-concept implementation of the proof-of-consent method, as described in chapter 6.

A.1   Initialisation module

```
<?

/* ISSUES
    # 1: if the user deleted the cookie and then tried to log-in again,
    the previous record in the session DB will not be deleted and a new session record
    will be created.
*/

$server = "DB server"; $db_user = "DB user"; $db_pass = "DB
password"; $database = "DB name";


####################################################################
```

```php
function fetch_substr_ip($ip)
{
    /*
    ipcheck
    0|255.255.255.255
    1|255.255.255.0
    2|255.255.0.0
    */
    $ipcheck = 1;
    return implode('.', array_slice(explode('.', $ip), 0, 4 - $ipcheck));
}
```

##

```php
function fetch_ip()
{
    return $_SERVER['REMOTE_ADDR'];
}
```

##

```php
function vbrand($min, $max) {
    $seed = (double) microtime() * 1000000;
    mt_srand($seed);
    return mt_rand($min, $max);
}
```

##

```php
Function ReDirectPage($message, $To){
    echo ("
<html> <head> <meta http-equiv=\"refresh\" content=\"6;URL=$To\">
</head> <body> <BR><BR><BR><BR> <div align=\"center\">
  <center>
  <table border=\"1\" cellpadding=\"0\" cellspacing=\"0\"
  style=\"border-collapse: collapse\" bordercolor=\"#111111\" width=\"80%\"
  id=\"AutoNumber1\" bgcolor=\"$tcolor1\">
```

```
  <tr>
    <td width=\"100%\" align=\"center\"><font size=4><B>
      $message
    </font></b></td>
    </tr>
  </table>
  </center>
</div> </body></html>"); } ?>
```

A.2 PoASet module

```php
<?php

include('init.php');

    $HOST = $_SERVER['REMOTE_ADDR'];
    $USERAGENT = $_SERVER['HTTP_USER_AGENT'];
    $SESSION_IDHASH = sha1($USERAGENT . fetch_substr_ip($HOST));
    $SESSION_HOST      = substr(fetch_ip(), 0, 15);
    $TIMENOW = time();
#
    $sessionhash = sha1($TIMENOW . $SESSION_IDHASH . $SESSION_HOST . vbrand(1, 1000000));
#
        $connection = @mysql_connect($server, $db_user, $db_pass) or
        die("Database Connection Error #: 100");
//      $query = "INSERT INTO session ('sessionhash', 'userid', 'host', 'idhash',
//      'lastactivity', 'useragent', 'loggedin') VALUES ('$sessionhash', '1', '$HOST',
//      $SESSION_IDHASH', '$TIMENOW', '$USERAGENT', '$TIMENOW');";
        $query = "INSERT INTO session VALUES ('$sessionhash', '1', '$HOST',
```

258

```
                '$SESSION_IDHASH', '$TIMENOW',

                '$USERAGENT', '$TIMENOW');";
//        echo $query. '<BR>';

                @mysql_db_query($database, $query) or die("ERROR DB on Create New Session D#101");

                @mysql_close($connection);
#
        setcookie("sessionhash", "$sessionhash", $TIMENOW + 3600, '/');
#
        ReDirectPage("Please Wait ...", "Homepage.php");
?>
```

A.3   PoACheck module

```
<?php

include('init.php');

if (!isset($_COOKIE["sessionhash"]))
    {
      echo ('Sorry you cannot use CardSpace this time, we have to ask you to enter
      your username and password');
      ReDirectPage($messege, "passwdcheck.php");
    }
    else
      {
        $OLD_sessionhash = $_COOKIE["sessionhash"];
        $HOST = $_SERVER['REMOTE_ADDR'];
        $USERAGENT = $_SERVER['HTTP_USER_AGENT'];
        $SESSION_IDHASH = sha1($USERAGENT . fetch_substr_ip($HOST));
```

259

```
    $SESSION_HOST =  substr(fetch_ip(), 0, 15);
    $TIMENOW = time();
#
    $connection = @mysql_connect($server, $db_user, $db_pass)
    or die("Database Connection Error #: 100");
    $result = @mysql_db_query($database, "SELECT * FROM session
    WHERE sessionhash = '$OLD_sessionhash'")
    or die("ERROR on Find Session DB#102");
      if (@mysql_num_rows($result) > 0){
        $db = mysql_fetch_array($result);
        if ($db[idhash] != $SESSION_IDHASH){
            setcookie("sessionhash", "", time()-3600, '/');
            $messege = "Uncorrect PoA! (Found in DB but from diffrent host). Sorry you cannot
            use CardSpace this time, we have to ask you to enter your username and password";
            ReDirectPage($messege, "passwdcheck.php");
            }
        else{//Update old session
            #
              $NEW_sessionhash = sha1($TIMENOW . $SESSION_IDHASH . $SESSION_HOST .
              vbrand(1, 1000000));
            #
                $connection = @mysql_connect($server, $db_user, $db_pass) or
                die("Database Connection Error #: 100");
//              $query = "INSERT INTO session ('sessionhash', 'userid', 'host', 'idhash',
//              'lastactivity', 'useragent', 'loggedin') VALUES ('$sessionhash', '1', '$HOST',
//              '$SESSION_IDHASH', '$TIMENOW', '$USERAGENT', '$TIMENOW');";
                $query = "UPDATE session SET sessionhash = '$NEW_sessionhash',
                lastactivity = '$TIMENOW' WHERE sessionhash = '$OLD_sessionhash';";
//              echo $query;
                @mysql_db_query($database, $query)
                or die("ERROR DB on Update New Session D#101");
                @mysql_close($connection);
            #
              setcookie("sessionhash", "$NEW_sessionhash", $TIMENOW + 3600, '/');
            #
```

```
                    `

                    echo "Correct PoA! We will proceed using CardSpace...";
                    ReDirectPage($messege, "CardSpace.php");
             }
       }
       else{
             setcookie("sessionhash", "", time()-3600, '/');
             $messege = "Uncorrect PoA! (Not Found in DB). Sorry you cannot use CardSpace
             this time, we have to ask you to enter your username and password";
             ReDirectPage($messege, "passwdcheck.php");
       }

}

?>
```